THE RETURN OF THE COMPLETE REVENGE KIT

by *Mark Leigh* and *Mike Lepine*

VIRGIN

First published in Great Britain in 1990 by
Virgin Books
A division of W. H. Allen & Co Plc
Sekforde House
175–9 St John Street
London EC1V 4LL

Designed by ACE Ltd

To Polly Leigh, who has decided that filling her nappy at 3.30 a.m. is an equally effective method of revenge.

Special thanks to: John Choopani, Craig Flint, Harrie Green, Philippa Hatton, Debbie Leigh, Chris Phillips, Graham Smith and Tracy Wheeler.

Other books by the same authors:

The Complete Revenge Kit
'Bitter and twisted.' *Over 21*
'The ultimate revenge for any situation.' *Campaign*

How To Be a Complete Bastard (with Adrian Edmondson)
'A sensitive, genteel little book.' *Daily Mirror*
'A monument to bad taste.' *Today*

How To Be a Complete Bitch (with Pamela Stephenson)
'Probably the most abusive and crude book written by a woman.' *Bath and West Evening Chronicle*
'Steamy, suggestive and laugh-a-minute.' *Celebrity*

The Book of Revelations

The Naughty 90s (published 1990)

ISBN 0-86369-337-7

Printed and bound in Great Britain by
Scotprint Ltd, Musselburgh, Scotland

Introduction

CHAPTER ONE

Revenge is Sweet . . .

They say there's ten million stories in the naked city.

Joe's was a tragedy.

Alone in his two-bit room, lit only by the flashing neon diner sign across the street, Joe hit his third bottle of T-bird wine with a vengeance. Like the other two, it shattered. Stupid move.

Nursing knuckles as bruised as his ego, Joe stared out on to the desolate, rain-lashed street below and recalled the sad train of events that had finally derailed him here, at the Heartbreak Hotel. He jammed his last Lucky into the corner of his mouth and attempted to strike a match, but it was too small a target and he missed.

Goddamn them all, every last one of them!

His so-called girlfriend who had stolen his heart – and then sold it to someone in a bar, *no questions asked*.

His so-called best friend who had stolen his girl – and then sold her to someone in a bar, *no questions asked*.

His so-called boss who had given him the big E – and then fired Joe when he caught him trying to sell it to someone in a bar, *no questions asked*.

All week, Joe had been plotting *revenge . . .*

And now, at last, he was ready.

Moving like a man with purpose once more, Joe turned on the light, slid home the chain on the hotel room door and carefully closed the blinds before sitting on the bed and slipping something out from beneath one of the stained pillows.

Embarrassed, he quickly put his lacy nylon nightie back again and reached under the *other* pillow for the brown paper bag that lay concealed beneath. With mounting excitement, his big calloused hands ripped open the bag to reveal a brand-new copy of *The Return of the Complete Revenge Kit*.

He recognised the authors' names immediately – *those two English guys with the huge dicks who had given bad taste a new name . . .**

Pausing only momentarily to caress its smooth exterior, Joe opened *The Return of the Complete Revenge Kit* and flicked through it, admiring its high production values and the myriad wonderful things you got for just £4.99.

Baffled only by the introduction, Joe realised immediately how to use the kit. Within two minutes he had selected three particularly cruel and vicious items, detaching them along the perforations with a cold precision, and then adding anonymous-looking signatures to make them look even more authentic.

The envelopes lay ready and waiting on the bedside table.

Joe smiled.

They say there's ten million stories in the naked city.

Maybe this one would have a happy ending, after all . . .

* ('Eric' – but it never caught on. Ed.)

MEET THE AUTHORS

NAME:	MIKE LEPINE	MARK LEIGH
AGE:	28	Twenty-something
MARITAL STATUS:	Single	Married but still frisky
PERSON MOST COMMONLY MISTAKEN FOR:	Trevor Eve or King Dong	Sebastian Coe or the 'Wimbledon Flasher'
IF NOT A WRITER, WHAT WOULD I BE:	Wealthier	The man who cuts off the electricity in old peoples' houses
PERSON I'D MOST LIKE TO BE:	Bruce Springsteen	Princess Di's gynaecologist
PERSON I'D LEAST LIKE TO BE:	Julian Clary	Benny Green's wife
FAVE FILM:	*The Exorcist*	*The Big Chill*
FAVE BOOK:	E. E. Cummings: *Complete Poems 1913–1962*	Argos Catalogue (Autumn 1987)
COMEDY INFLUENCES:	Monty Python; Woody Allen; Renwick & Marshall; David Nobbs	*MAD* magazine; Woody Allen when he was funny
PERSON I'D MOST LIKE TO HAVE A ROMANTIC FLING WITH:	Debbie Greenwo . . . Ow! Ow! Ow! I mean, my present girlfriend . . .	Mike's present girlfrie . . . Ow! Ow! Ow! I mean, Debbie Greenwood . . .
PERSON I'D MOST LIKE TO FEED HEAD FIRST INTO A GIANT LIQUIDISER:	75% of those currently employed in the publishing industry	Sue Lawley
LIKES:	Bruce Springsteen; cigarettes, whisky and wild, wild women	Orange jelly with mandarin segments in it; people who buy my books; publishers and agents who pay on time
DISLIKES:	Everything else	Jazz; fundamentalism; the kids from *Fame*; Pizza Hut getting a takeaway order incorrect (i.e. 9 times out of 10)
FAVE PLANET:	Pluto (it's far out . . .)	Uranus (ooh, er)
MOST MEMORABLE MOMENT IN WRITING CAREER:	*Bastard* getting to No. 1 at Christmas 1986	Turning down the chance to write *The Satanic Verses*
WORST TIME AT SCHOOL:	1972–7	10.47 a.m.
NAME OF CHILDHOOD SWEETHEART:	Dawn Austin	Eric
INVENTIONS THAT I COULD LIVE WITHOUT:	Marxism; Fashion; Cricket; Nouvelle Cuisine; Country Pubs	The penis enlarger
FAVE SHAPE:	Thin	Belinda Carlisle
FUNNIEST WORD:	Bollocks!	Ringpiece

SOCIETY FOR THE PREVENTION OF NOISE POLLUTION

Established 1903

National Headquarters:
4th Floor, Silvertree Buildings,
Minton Road,
E. Finchley,
London NW8 TT4

Date as postmark

Telephone: 01-490 0688 or
071-490 0688

Dear Sir and Madam

A number of complaints have been passed to this office, relating to the matter of disturbing noises originating from your property.

The plaintiffs all cite the problem as being 'the sounds of loud, persistent, aggressive, protracted and abandoned lovemaking' at varying hours of the evening, and have asked us to intervene on their behalf.

Many couples don't realise that, in their most private moments, they can often be heard up to 650 feet away, through walls, windows, ceilings or floors, and that the sounds of lovemaking can be disturbing and distressing to children and small pets, as well as deeply offensive to the elderly or religious.

Most couples, when they do realise the situation, find suitable ways around the problem. For example, many couples find that the act of wearing a gag during the act can actually heighten the excitement. Biting the pillow is also an excellent solution, as is making love in a fully insulated loft or attic.

Rest assured, this is a fairly common complaint, and the society deals with somewhere in the region of 5,000 such cases every year. We believe that matters of this kind can be handled satisfactorily by a simple letter of complaint, rather than bringing the matter to the attention of the court, with all the inevitable publicity which may then ensue.

However, should you feel inclined to ignore this warning, we will have no option but to ask the court to invoke local ordinances preventing you, by penalty of law, from making love between the hours of 8 pm and 7 am.

In anticipation of your compliance.

Yours sincerely

Honorary Fellow

From Santa's Workshop

Dear

Your mummy and daddy have told me not to bring any presents to you this year unless you do all the washing up, hoover the living room, dig the garden, wash the car, go down the road and do all the shopping, tidy your room and have your pocket money cut in half.

Well, there you have it. Take it or leave it.

Love
Santa XXX

From Santa's Workshop

Dear

I would love to put your presents in your stocking again this year, but the rampaging, throat-slitting, totally evil bogie man who lives in *your wardrobe* nearly ripped my bollocks off last year.

Is it alright if I leave them under your tree instead?

Love
Santa XXX

From Santa's Workshop

Dear

I am afraid that I'm only going to give presents to pretty boys and girls this year.

So you're not going to get any.

Love
Santa XXX

From Santa's Workshop

Dear

I am afraid that I will not be bringing you any toys this year because I don't really exist.

Yours
Santa XXX

D E N S A

National Headquarters: 17/19 Herbert Place, London SW17 TL4
Telephone: 01-490 0688 or 071-490 0688

Dear

Thank you for filling out the coupon in one of the Sunday rags inviting you to join D.E.N.S.A. and asking for more gen so you can suss out whether or not you ought to join.

What is D.E.N.S.A.? Well, for far to long those bright boffin types have had things all there own way! They think they're the bee's knees and they've even got they're own club which we can't join.

Well, if they've got a club why shouldn't we? Just because were not inteligent doesn't mean were stupid . . . so D.E.N.S.A. is the club for you and me - ordinary people who haven't swallowed a dictionary or think that doing sums is a good crack!

You don't have to pass any tests, and being a member of D.E.N.S.A. has some real good advantages, like:

* Parties!!
* Cut-price subscriptions to *The Sun*!
* Club hols to Spain, Corfu . . . and lots of other really great places!
* Tickets to see top TV progs ACTUALLY BEING MADE . . .stuff like *3-2-1, Blind Date and Telly Addicts*!!!
* Vintage London-to-Luton Ford Capri rallies!
* Regular knees-ups at some of London's hottest nightspots!!!
* Free lager tastings!!!
* Ladies only XXXX hen nights with naughty cabarets!!!
* Pets club gives you whopping savings on pit bulls and rottweilers!
* Free legal advice on dealing with the council and the social.
* Free signed pickie of BOBBY DAVRO!!!
* Neat discounts on all Stock Aitken Waterman hits!
* Snooker and darts comps for big cash prizes!
* Cut-priced tickets to *The Cannon and Ball Show*!
* Free!!! Six steamy pics of Maria Whittaker (lads only!)
* Free!!! Steamy pics of heart-throb Jason Donovan (ladies only)

So come on in! It's like being among your mates!

Membership is only £21 a year . . . less than twenty pints of best! Weve run out of application forms at the mo, because demand to join is so high, but if you want to join, just give me a tinkle on the number above. See ya soon!

Cheers

Membership Secretary

President: Wayne Stoppard. Vice President: Kevin Trotter. Treasurer: Gavin Whittles. Secretary: Tracey Bates. Membership Secretary: Shazza Gormley. Honorary Members: Chris Quenntin, Ian Bowtham, Sinnita, Jim Davison.

METHATECH LTD

ALTERNATIVE ENERGY APPLIANCES FOR THE HOME

12/16 Morking Street, London NE10 TL4.
Telephone: 01-490 0688 or 071-490 0688

Ref: TH/433/fd

Date as postmark

Dear Madam

Thank you for your recent enquiry about the new SEPTON 5000 combined septic tank and oven, and requesting a no-obligation ten-day trial.

As pioneers in the use of methane as a alternate energy source for the home, we will be pleased to install the SEPTON 5000 next Tuesday morning as arranged. It will be yours for a ten-day period, during which time you'll see the great energy savings that can be made.

The waste tank is manufactured in easy-to-clean white UPVC and at only 3'6" high and 2' wide (approx 107 cms x 61 cms) is discreet enough to blend with any kitchen decor, and the built-in oven means that there is no unsightly external pipework.

Once installed, operation is simplicity itself.

The human and animal waste is inserted through a small hatch at the top of the unit. The methane gas produced as the waste decomposes is channelled directly to the oven via a catalytic convertor which removes most of the impurities.

The oven itself features automatic piezo-ignition, and thermostatic control ensures perfect results every time - your family won't even notice the characteristic smell after a few days!

The SEPTON 5000 is well proven. We manufacture here in the UK and export all over the world. In Turkey alone, over 130,000 women cook on a SEPTON 5000; proof indeed that the future of cooking is SEPTON.

See you next Tuesday.

Yours sincerely

Customer Liaison Manager

P.S. As a special limited offer we'll be giving you a three-month 'starter pack' of animal waste to get your cooking under way. There's no obligation - the waste is yours to keep whether you return the SEPTON 5000 or not!

BAR CODE BONANZA! ! !

||||||||||||||||||||||||||||||||||||||||||||||||||||||||||||||||||||||||

NOBODY LIKES GOING TO THE SUPERMARKET, BUT NOW HERE'S A WAY TO MAKE IT MORE ENJOYABLE - BY WINNING YOUR WEEK'S SHOPPING ABSOLUTELY FREE!

THE ASSOCIATION OF SUPERMARKETS ANNOUNCES A UNIQUE COMPETITION: **THE BAR CODE BONANZA !**

AND IT COULDN'T BE SIMPLER TO ENTER !

TAKE THIS LETTER WITH ITS UNIQUE BAR CODE WITH YOU THE NEXT TIME YOU VISIT YOUR PARTICIPATING SUPERMARKET. THEN PRESENT IT TO THE CASHIER WITH YOUR SHOPPING.

SHE'LL PASS IT OVER THE SCANNER AND IF IT GOES 'BLEEP-BLEEP-BLEEP' YOUR SHOPPING (UP TO A VALUE OF £100) WILL COST YOU £1 ! YES, £1 !

400,000 BAR CODES HAVE BEEN DISTRIBUTED AND OVER 12,000 CONTAIN A POTENTIAL WINNING CODE, SO YOU HAVE A GREAT CHANCE OF WINNING !! AND THE WINNING CODE IS CHANGED EVERY DAY - SO THE MORE YOU SHOP, THE GREATER YOUR CHANCES !!

REMEMBER, IF THE BAR CODE GOES BLEEP-BLEEP-BLEEP - YOUR SHOPPING IS CHEAP-CHEAP-CHEAP !!

Conditions of entry

1. Only one winning bar code may be redeemed per customer (this becomes the property of the supermarket).
2. Only goods presented at the same time as the bar code are eligible for the competition.
3. Alcohol and cigarettes are excluded from the competition and, in the case of a winning bar code, must be paid for separately.
4. Closing date: 31 July 1992.

To the retailer

Customers with a winning bar code are entitled to their shopping at the time of presentation of the bar code free up to a value of £100.

Alcohol and cigarettes are excluded from this total.

Winning bar codes should be retained with a copy of the receipt and forwarded to your Association of Supermarkets representative for rebate.

Phone 01-490 0688 or 071-490 0688 for further details.

THE PRIVATE MEDICAL TRUST

SERVING THE COMMUNITY SINCE 1976

The Bellwood Clinic, Hunt Place, London W2 TL4. Telephone: 01-490 0688 or 071-490 0688

Date as postmark

Dear

Thank you for your enquiry, regarding donating organs to the Private Medical Trust's Organ Donor Bank.

When you fill out a Private Organ Donor Card, you can be sure that your vital organs will only go to someone who *really* matters, instead of just anybody (who, after all, might be a criminal or worse!).

All those on our books awaiting transplants are wealthy, highly successful men and women, well respected in their fields and with a positive contribution to make - many are even titled!

Among our clientele we number judges and magistrates, managing directors, senior politicians, country gentry, publishers, masters of hounds, masonic dignitaries, socialites and private investors - the very backbone of Britain!

And look at the difference! If you carry an ordinary donor card, your relatives get NOTHING in the event of your death. But with PMT's Organ Donor Card, they'll receive up to £20,000 per usable organ within just forty-eight hours - because, unlike the dregs on the NHS, our clients can PAY - and pay heftily!

A Private Organ Donor Card will be despatched within the next forty-eight hours by first-class post. However, with regard to the point raised in your letter, I am afraid to say we cannot purchase one eye from you whilst you are still alive. However, it is perfectly possible for us to negotiate the purchase of one lung and/or kidney and our regional sales representative will call upon you shortly to negotiate terms and thereafter arrange the operation at a clinic convenient to you.

Thanking you again for your enquiry.

Yours sincerely

Assistant Medical Administrator

BRAZILIAN CONSULAR OFFICE

17 Bonden Street, London W1 TT4.
Telephone: 01-490 0688 or 071-490 0688 (extension 398)

Dear Sir/Madam

It has come to our attention that you have links with our nation due to a blood relative currently residing in Brazil.

Under the 1968 Military Service Act you are bound by the Anglo- Brazilian Treaty to serve a period of two consecutive years in the Brazilian Army.

In the first instance, please register at the Brazilian Consulate on the date shown below. Arrangements will then be made for your transportation to Brazil. If there is any valid reason why you should be ineligible for military service, please bring all supporting documents with you.

Registration at Consulate: _____ (date) am/pm

Failure to respond to this notification of draft will result in summary custody and full house arrest by the Brazilian military police. Extradition proceedings will then be expedited in the courts.

Thanking you in advance for your co-operation,

Julio Colombos Y Fuego
Military Attache

GALLETAS SURTIDAS IMPORTADAS

DEPARTMENT OF ENVIRONMENTAL WELFARE AND HEALTH

39 Ornington Mews, Ornington Street, London W1 TL4.
Telephone: 01-490 0688 or 071- 490 0688

Date as postmark

Dear Sir/Madam

It has come to our attention that you are feeding birds (and possibly other wildlife) by depositing foodstuffs on land immediately adjoining your property.

It is our duty to inform you that this continued action constitutes an offence under the 1989 Wildlife Protection Act. This law makes it illegal to provide food for birds unless an Aviary Catering Licence is applied for and granted.

Although not common knowledge, the Wildlife Protection Act was passed in order to control the rapidly increasing numbers of selected UK breeds (including the House Sparrow, Mistle Thrush, Rook, Robin, Pigeon, Chaffinch and Starling), which constitute a public health hazard and nuisance because of their dependence on discarded rubbish and waste.

cont.

This control over their numbers has been necessary to restore the balance of nature and ensure that the food-chain remains stable.

An Aviary Catering Licence is available from your local post office at a cost of £5 per annum (ask for form 54L). Continued feeding of birds without a licence is a criminal offence and, if proven, can result in a fine of up to £200.

Thanking you for your co-operation

Regional Environmental Health Officer

PRODUCTS ON PARADE!

A NEW SERVICE FROM DOOR-TO-DOOR DEALINGS LTD.

National Offices: 3rd Floor, Charlton Plaza, Bolland Street, London NW4 TL4. Telephone: 01-490 0688 or 071-490 0688

Dear Householder

Our records show that at some time in the past you've taken advantage of the ease and convenience of shopping from home. It might have been by mail order, or by telephone, or from a visiting salesman.

Either way, you now know just how pleasant it is to do your shopping from home - away from the bustle and the crowds and the inevitable queues - so we know you'll be delighted to participate in an exciting event being held in your area next week!

It's called 'PRODUCTS ON PARADE' - and the thinking behind it is extremely simple! Instead of you going to the shops, WE'LL BRING THE SHOPS TO YOU! Imagine the convenience (not to mention the SAVINGS on bus and train fares!).

Starting at _____ am on _____day, you'll be visited by trained sales representatives showing you beautiful and useful items. They might be gifts, or delicious foods, or useful household utensils - and you can peruse them all WITH NO OBLIGATION!! YES, EVERY TWENTY MINUTES, a sales representative will call on you for a FULL DAY of thrilling shopping from home!!!

Here are just a few of the exciting PRODUCTS ON PARADE you'll get to see!
* Dustotronic 2000 carpet sweepers
* Blenheim Military Book Club
* Tipson's Foods (delicious blancmange mixes from around the globe!)
* Natchworth Fitted Kitchens
* The S.D.L.P.
* Raki's Insurance Co PLC
* Nicklin and McKay Drainage Consultants PLC
* Findlay's Double Glazing
* Mackies' Household Dusters and Cleaning Agents
* The Jehovah's Witnesses
* Drummond's Family Encyclopedias (A paroxysm of information on the page!)
* Rock Bottom Insurance Co Ltd
* Goebbel-Strauss Investment Consultants
* The Salvation Army
* Household utensils *par excellence* from Hotchworths
* Sizzlers 'Adult' Novelties
* O'Toole's House Extensions and Renovations Ltd
* Derby's Deluxe Fitted Bathrooms
* Knight's Super Hankies
* Proserpine Shield Life Assurance and Endowment Specialists
* Peters and Bloch (tank-lagging our speciality!!)
* Janey's Snakes 'n' Lizards

And those are just some of the highlights of your great day shopping from home.

Be sure you're in! If you can't make that time, call us up and we'll reschedule you. AND DON'T WORRY IF YOU FORGET ABOUT US AND ACCIDENTALLY GO OUT ON THAT DAY! PRODUCTS ON PARADE is going to be in your area for some time to come, so we can drop in and surprise you!!

Enjoy yourself!

Sales Co-ordinator

DEPARTMENT OF LEGALISED REGISTRATION

4 Oxbridge Road, London W1 TL4. Telephone: 01-490 0688 or 071-490 0688 Ext. 51

Our ref: TF/270/L
Your ref: 41/MK

Dear Sir or Madam
Deportation Order

In the routine computerisation of our existing records, it has come to light that you are one of twenty direct descendants of Mr Johann Christian Mittermaier, who entered this country and settled here illegally from the Principality of Anhalt-Dessau in 1714.

Nationality as a full British subject is established in one of two ways: birthright, which is defined as parentage by two full British subjects; or through legal and permitted entry and subsequent qualification. As your ancestor did not establish any such rights to become a subject of the United Kingdom, its Commonwealth or Protectorates, his descendants are similarly not subjects of the aforementioned territories and have no rights of residence therein.

Notice is hereby given that you must cease to reside in the territories of the United Kingdom, its Commonwealth and Protectorates within ninety days, surrendering your passport to the relevant authorities at your point of departure. Whilst your husband or wife (if you are married) retains full rights of residence, such children as you may have, in that they are full descendants, will similarly share your loss of citizenship and must leave with you.

Whilst it is not the province of this Department to proffer a place of residence, it should be noted that your ancestors possessed full citizenship of Anhalt-Dessau. This German Principality was subsumed into the greater Germany during the nineteenth century and now forms part of East Germany. The authorities of the aforementioned state may, of course, not recognise rights of citizenship dating back to the eighteenth century. It is up to you to take matters further.

Should you wish to lodge an appeal against this ruling, as is your right, you should do so within the next seven days by telephoning the number above for an appointment. It should be noted, however, that over 95% of all appeals are overturned as the laws relating to this area are well defined and tested in due process.

Your compliance with all aspects of, and in relation to, this letter is appreciated.

Yours faithfully

Higher Executive Officer

Dear _____,

I AM CHUCKING YOU BECAUSE . . .

• I never really loved you. It was just infatuation. [ ]
• Your dick's too small for anything permanent. [ ]
• I can't spend the rest of my life with a man hung like a squirrel. [ ]
• You're sick. [ ]
• I don't fancy being Mrs Pathetic Little Wimp in a couple of years. [ ]
• I couldn't inflict your looks on our children. [ ]
• You're just not good enough. [ ]
• I've only been going out with you to hide my biker boyfriend from [ ]
  my parents.
• I decided it wasn't fair to keep cheating on you any longer. [ ]
• I'm sick of all my friends laughing at me. [ ]
• I've found out what I've been missing. [ ]
• I've discovered God and I know now that it's immoral to go out [ ]
  with someone purely for their money.
• I'm bored with you. You're a prick, now shove off. [ ]
• I've become allergic to greasy little prats. [ ]
• I know that you love me more than life itself but I've decided I [ ]
  want to give my body to lots and lots of other men and have one-
  night stands and sleep with Spanish waiters who mean nothing
  to me on holiday so you can't ever hear 'Dolce Vita' or 'La Isla
  Bonita' again without doubling up in pain and then give my all to
  painters and decorators and mechanics to whom I'm less than dirt
  just for kicks and, well, I think you get the picture . . .
• Your best friend showed me what deep and sweaty physical love [ ]
  between two people is all about.
• I love you, but you haven't got a Lamborghini, so this is goodbye. [ ]
• I've got to get out now, before you put me off all men. [ ]
• Your eyes clash with my mascara. [ ]
• You should have bought me that car when I asked for it. [ ]

Yours

_____

P.S. DON'T YOU DARE DO ANY OF THE FOLLOWING:

* Come round.
* Phone me.
* 'Accidentally' bump into me.
* Go sobbing to my best friend, hoping she'll put in a good word for
   you.
* Try the same routine on my parents.
* Tell me you're going to kill yourself - because I don't have an IQ
   under fifty.
* Promise me things will be different next time.
* Tell everyone you chucked me, because I told them all what I was
   going to do a month ago.
* Tell your mates how useless I was in bed, because most of them
   know it isn't true.

INVITATION

Dear . . . . and . . . . ,
I'm having a 'Tarts & Tramps' fancy dress party on
. . . . at . . . .
and I'd really like you both to be there.
Love. . . . .

R.S.V.P.

P.S. Come as you are.

INVITATION

Dear . . . .
I'm having a Seventies theme party on. . . . . at . . . . .
. . . .
It should be perfect for you because you won't need to hire
any special costumes.
Love. . . . .

R.S.V.P.

INVITATION

Dear . . . .
A party wouldn't be a party without you! Who else is there
who gets pissed after two glasses of punch and spends the rest
of the evening slam-dancing to Alexander O'Neal,
regurgitating the buffet at least twice and ending up crashed
out in the bathroom with their knickers on their head? I do
hope you can make it on. . . . . at . . . .
. . . .
Love. . . . .

R.S.V.P.

LAMB LANE FARM

London Offices:
14 St Adrian's Lane
London WC4 TT4
Telephone: 01-490 0688
or 071-490 0688

Duburton Lane
The Shunt
Crigsley
Derbyshire
DR7 VL2

Dear

Regarding your letter of the 16th, I regret to inform
you that it is not the policy of this farm to sell sheep
to individuals.

All our stock is sold at auction to registered meat
traders with whom we enjoy an excellent relationship.

We would certainly not - from anyone - accept an order
that specified a sheep 'capable of fitting into a size
eight dress' nor one requesting an animal which is, to
quote your letter, 'more passive and docile perhaps than
its compatriots in the flock, sweet-tempered yet frisky
by nature but willing to hold still when commanded . .
and which doesn't bleat very loudly even under the most
gross of provocations, such that it might betray its
presence to all and sundry in the locality'.

Furthermore, we regret that we cannot recommend any
other farming establishment or 'sheep enthusiasts' club'
from which you might be able to procure a sheep.

Might I suggest that you seek further help in this
matter elsewhere.

Yours sincerely

Head of Livestock

THE BELLWOOD CLINIC

15 - 24 Cromwell Place. London SW7 TL1. Telephone: 01-490 0688 or 071-490 0688
Ref: 3435/FR/3

Date as postmark

Dear Sir

This letter confirms that all the necessary arrangements have
been made for your forthcoming sex change operation next week.

I must say, during my time as registrar at the Bellwood
Clinic, this is the first time anyone has opted for a local
anaesthetic. Dr Lerner is pleased to facilitate your request
and is confident that pain will be minimal.

Although your pre-med will not be until next Wednesday morning
at 9.30, Dr Lerner will be visiting you at home this Friday
with the final consent forms and to finalise the type of
breasts you would like. Given your physique he sees no reason
why a 34B would not be feasible.

Regarding the removal of your sexual organs, it is the
clinic's practice to dispose of these in our incinerator. From
time to time, however, we do have requests for these to be
saved and preserved in a saline solution 'for old time's
sake'.

Could you let De Lerner know your requirements so that the
necessary arrangements can be made in advance.

Yours sincerely

Chief Registrar

P.S. The full body electrolysis treatment will take two days,

The Bellwood Clinic is a member of the F.D.M.B.C.

CENTRALE BUREAU DE POSTE EUROPEEN

Poste-Europe, 2541 Rue Plagier, Bruxelles 42387.   AMI Buildings, St Adrian's Lane, London W1 TL4.

Telephone: 01-490 0688 or 071-490 0688

Dear Householder

As 1992 approaches, letter boxes everywhere are to be standardised to facilitate the swift and efficient flow of post between member states of the European Community.

In line with Euro Post Office Directive 14K/21/PO/S1 issued by the Postburghermeister's office, letter boxes within the UK must now all be adapted to a standard Eurosize of 89.4 cm deep by 25.6 cm wide.

If your letter box does not meet this requirement, you should act now to assure the continued delivery of your post by having suitable alterations made. These can be carried out by yourself or by any certified Eurocarpenter or Letter Box Operative. And - if you are a low-income family - you may be entitled to have conversion work carried out free of charge (ask for form 1/4/AFD at your local post office).

A variety of attractive, exterior metal fascias will be available to decorate your new letter box, including representations of Charles De Gaulle, Topo Giggio, the Right Honourable Edward Heath and a full selection of famous Belgian statesmen, including of course Jacques Cessoirre.

Doorbells will also be standardised to fit in with the theme of a single market and to facilitate the delivery of registered mail and larger packages. Ask at your local post office for an illustrated leaflet and more information on the full range of Eurofascias and doorbells available.

Thank you for your co-operation, which will ensure that our new Euro Post Service will continue to uphold the same standard of quality and speed of delivery that you have come to expect from your own national post office.

Date as postmark

UK Offices:
34 Gillburton Street,
London W9 RL3.
Telephone:
01-490 0688 or
071-490 0688

Dear Franchisee

LOCATION OF NEW FRANCHISE

Welcome aboard! We're pleased to say that your
application to own and manage your own PISA PIZZA
restaurant has been accepted. We've received verbal
agreement that your bank loan has been secured; all we're
waiting for now is written notification. However, we usually
regard that as merely a formality.

As you know, owners of PISA PIZZA franchises enjoy all the benefits
of working for themselves, but with all the business expertise,
support and back-up of a large company behind them.

Support like a staff training scheme, free uniforms, national
advertising support, bulk buying facilities and extended credit.

We will begin work next Monday on converting your premises to follow
the corporate design of all PISA PIZZA restaurants. Our contracts
department will take care of all the details, including planning
permission for the two 3m high 'Leaning Tower' neon signs that will
be installed each side of the entrance.

It is estimated that this work will take a week, after which the
wiring and plumbing will be connected. Once the fridges and ovens
are up and running we will deliver the first stocks - enough dough,
mozzarella cheese, tomatoes and assorted toppings to serve 2,200
Crusty Pan and 1,250 Thin Slice pizzas; and enough vegetables for
970 side salads, plus 450 gallons of assorted soft drinks and 80 lb
of freeze-dried coffee.

You'll be open for business within two weeks of receiving this
letter - that's how fast near you are to becoming your own boss!

See you Monday morning, and, as we say, *buona fortuna!*

FRANCHISES
THROUGHOUT
THE UK AND
EUROPE

Franchise Manager

Smythe & Wagner

Auctioneers By Appointment Since 1709

3rd Floor, Duburton Buildings, St Angus Lane, London W1 TL4
Telephone: 01-490 0688 or 071-490 0688

Date as postmark

Dear

I am writing to inform you that your postal bid for government surplus lot G.HMSO.249 has been successful at auction and that you are now the sole legal owner of said lot.

May we now confirm where you would like the submarine to be delivered?

Being a 1944 M-class vessel of some 3,000 imperial tonnes and spanning 76 feet from bow to stern, it would not appear feasible for you to store HMS *Apollo* at your given address, which is obviously residential in nature, prior to dismantling it for scrap metal. However, unless we receive written confirmation of an alternative delivery address within seven days, we shall comply with the instructions on your postal bid. Relocation of said lot will thereafter be your sole responsibility.

In compliance with our usual terms and conditions, you will be invoiced for the full amount of the bid (plus VAT at 15% and agent's commission at 7.5%) on receipt of the vessel. Personal cheques, we regret, cannot be accepted, even with a cheque guarantee card. Instead, payment should be in the form of a banker's draft, building society cheque or pounds sterling.

May we take this opportunity to thank you for participating in the auction and assure you of our very best service at all times.

Yours sincerely

Senior Partner

THE BELLWOOD CLINIC

15 - 24 Cromwell Place, London SW7 TL1. Telephone: 01-490 0688 or 071-490 0688

Date as postmark

Dear Sir

Since 1975 it has been mandatory upon us to seek and receive the husband's written consent and approval prior to proceeding with any operation, under penalty of law.

We would therefore ask you to reply in writing within twenty-one days, stating that you consent to your wife undergoing a gender swapping operation, and further indemnifying us against any future action arising from the operation.

As you are well aware, your wife has undergone stringent clinical tests and results show that there will be no complications in what is now considered a fairly minor operation.

She has completed all the consent forms and we are only awaiting your reply to this letter before confirming the date of her admittance to this clinic.

I look forward to hearing from you on this matter at your earliest convenience.

Yours faithfully

Chief Administrator

The Bellwood Clinic is a member of the F.D.M.B.C.

THE WOMEN'S EDUCATIONAL TRUST

Founded 1917

National Offices: The Dell, 51 Agaten Street, London W1 TT4. Telephone: 01-490 0688 or 071-490 0688

Dear

Thank you very much for your kind invitation to host a slide show and lecture for our local Women's Educational Trust group in your home.

The theme of your talk - 'The History, Development and Cultural Meaning of the Hurdy-Gurdy Man' - sounds most edifying, and I must report that we have to date sold over seventeen tickets for this event.

Your collection of slides, including pictures taken at the 1957 Festivo de Hurdy-Gurdy de Barcelona, Barry 'Mr Hurdy-Gurdy' Burnett captured live at the Glasgow Empire in 1931 and the recent Covent Garden Hurdy-Gurdython for children's charities, would seem most fascinating - and I am sure we are all in for what will be a most memorable evening!

In my dual capacity as acting chairperson of the catering sub-committee, I will be arranging the tea and biscuits, so there is no need to trouble yourself to provide anything by way of refreshments.

Once again, thank you for kindly offering to give your talk to our group. I look forward to meeting you in person next Thursday at 7.30 pm.

Yours sincerely

Chairperson

OVER 600 BRANCHES THROUGHOUT THE UNITED KINGDOM

THE NATIONAL SOCIETY FOR THE CARE AND REHABILITATION OF TORTOISES

FOUNDED 1915

Patron: HRH Prince Terence of Gloucester

Registered Offices:
18 McIver Park Place, London SW14 TT4. Telephone: 01-490 0688 or 071-490 0688

Dear

I am writing to confirm receipt of your direct debit instruction to your bank on behalf of the N.S.C.R.T.

Starting from next month, your salary will automatically be transferred from your bank account into the N.S.C.R.T. account on the first Monday of each month.

May I take this opportunity, on behalf of the N.S.C.R.T. and the some 4,000 tortoises, turtles and terrapins in our care, to thank you for this act of generosity.

Helping the tortoise may not seem like such an important charity when weighed against some of the problems that beset the world today, but be assured that, without proper care, tortoises can experience severe levels of suffering. Without our hothouses, for example - which are paid for entirely by contributions from members of the public like yourself - tortoises would be exposed to an alien British climate which could lead them to being unresponsive, sullen and withdrawn, completely devoid of the usual playfulness and *joie de vivre* one usually associates with a healthy, well-adjusted tortoise.

Your contribution will also help to pay for our rehabilitation programme, which intends to return some 2,000 domestic tortoises back into the wilds over the next five years, with a learning programme to help them redevelop their predatory hunting instincts and to fit in seamlessly with the complex mores and laws which govern tortoise society in the wild.

Thank you again for your generous patronage.

Yours sincerely

Vice Administrator

Dear 'Glenda',

I heard you on Radio 1's sexual problem phone-in last week and
~~appreciatex~~ appreciate you giving out your name and full postal
address live on air. That was a very brave ~~gesture~~ gesture, especially since transvestites like ourselves are so often widely
    persecuted and ~~villified~~ when we 'come out of the wardrobe', so
to speak.

I was excited to hear your plans to start a self- help group in
this area and I'm looking forward to the first meeting next Sunday
afternoon at your house. As you said, the more the merrier, so I'm
bringing along two of my friends, Jacqui and Lolita, who are also
into cross -dressing in a big way.

 As you said on-air, we transvestites really need to bring our
secret into the open, and educating the public is what it's all
about, despite the ~~dersio~~ derision and physical violence we've come
to expect - not to mention the hazards of being sacked from work
once the secret gets around.

The idea of inviting all your neighbours to a garden party at some
point in the future - to show them that transvestites are ordinary
people, too, as you so ~~elaquant~~ eloquently put it -- sounds great
and Jacqui, Lolita and I are all looking forward to showing off
our new frocks and matching accessories.

You're really fortunate that the woman in your life understands you.
Mine left me after eight years of marriage, taking with her our
daughter and an absolutely scrumptious wardrobe- this seems to be an
occupational hazard of our way of life.

Anyway, see you Sunday afternoon,

Erica (Eric)

P.S. My telephone number's 01-490 0688 (or 071-490 0688), if you
want to give me a bell.

Sorry, you were out when we called. Please phone us to arrange another appointment.

ROCKLAND IRVING AND MINSK

Solicitors
Specialists in Divorce Proceedings

40 Fortenby Mews, Germain Street, London W2 TL4.
Telephone: 01-490 0688 or 071-490 0688

Sorry, you were out when I called. Please telephone to arrange another appointment.

Ms Jacqui Dortmund F.Sci, Dip Med

CONTACT

Sexual Therapy Clinic

Telephone: 01-490 0688 or 071-490 0688

Sorry, you were out when we called. Please telephone us to arrange another appointment.

SWEET DREAMS

*UNWANTED AND UNLOVED PETS HUMANELY PUT TO SLEEP
DISTANCE NO OBJECT*

Sorry, you were out when we called. Please telephone us to arrange another appointment.

The Betty Hubbard Clinic

Fast, discreet pregnancy testing at home

The Squirey, 47 Richelieu Place, London WC2 TL4.
Telephone: 01-490 0688 or 071-490 0688

Sorry, you were out when we called. Please telephone us to arrange another appointment.

TRANSVESTITE SUPPORT SCHEME

Sympathetic, private counselling
and aversion therapy in the home.

Telephone: 01-490 0688 or 071-490 0688 (24 hours)

Sorry, you were out when we called. Please telephone us to arrange another appointment.

POTENTIAL

Discreet, professional calculation of
sperm count in the home.

The Bellwood Clinic, Robbins Lane, London NW2 TL4.
Telephone: 01-490 0688 or 071-490 0688

HORNY HOLS LTD

Directors: K.Smith, G.F.Smith, A.Vishwani

2nd Floor, 11 Chigley Street, London E8 TT4. Telephone: 01-490 0688 or 071-490 0688

Date as postmark

Dear

Thanks for asking for our 'Bangkok Breaks' brochure. Unfortunately, our holidays are SO POPULAR we've run out of brochures at the moment, but let me tell you a bit more about what you can expect on a 'Horny Hols' tour!

Horny Hols specialises in holidays for the older bachelor (or the married man who can slip away from her indoors and the kids for a week or so). And the fun starts as soon as you get on board the charter flight - all our stewardesses are COMPLETELY TOPLESS!

Touch down in Bangkok (or Phuket on our fourteen-day breaks) and you'll find young, dusky, hot'n'ready babes just waiting for <u>YOU!</u>

You can be old, paunchy, balding, wrinkly, toothless - THEY DON'T CARE!!! (In fact, they seem to like it better!!! Wow!) YOU CAN'T FAIL TO SCORE . . . AGAIN . . . AND AGAIN . . . AND AGAIN!!!! (Better pack those heart pills!!)

And we'll show you the hottest spots in town - and we MEAN the HOTTEST! Some of the fabulous hi-lights of your tour will be:

* The Red Puppy Club's amazing 'Hide The Chicken' floorshow (XXXXX!)
* The world-famous Dollar Club - where woman meets lobster!
* Barney's all-girl display (how DO they do it - and who cleans up afterwards????)
* The London Bar's 'Nudey Banana Relay Marathon - (you'll never see tropical fruits in the same light again!)
* Bangkok's 5-star 'Restaurant de Femmes', where men are men - and women are crockery

Our prices include everything but the bints - and with poverty the way it is in Thailand, you can pick them up for less than a pint of best back home!!!

So you're guaranteed a really stonk-a-thonic time, because no matter how skint you are, they're skinter still!!!

Choose from our three-day mini break, our seven-day Bankok tour or our fourteen-day two-centre (Phuket and Bankok) deluxe tour of a lifetime (it's less of a holiday - and more of an endurance test!!!).

Prices include flights, all meals and accommodation - as well as our own medical facilities to spare.you the embarrassment of consulting your family doctor - and holidays start from just £517 off-season!

If you can't wait for our brochure to arrive, pick up the phone and call us right now! And give yourself the treat of a lifetime!!!

Yours sincerely

Director

CENTRAL COMMUNITY CHARGE
ADMINISTRATIVE OFFICE

AMI Buildings, St Adrian's Lane, London W1 TL4
Telephone: 01-490 0688 or 071-490 0688

Date as postmark

Dear Occupier

Further to Amendment 34/2 recently passed to the legal provision for the collection of the Community Charge (more commonly referred to as the 'Poll Tax'), certain household pets must now be included for the purposes of assessment.

Those household pets defined as having free run of your property and its facilities, such as cats and dogs, are now liable to pay the Community Charge at $^1/_3$ rd rate.

Caged animals, such as small rodents and marsupials and birds, are exempt and zero-rated, as they are not at liberty to enjoy the full facilities of the domicile.

If you are in any doubt as to which category any animal in your possession falls into, you should contact your local town hall immediately. *Remember that failure to register all occupants of your residence for the Community Charge can constitute a criminal offence.*

If you have a pet which qualifies for the Community Charge, please complete the form below, detach it and return it to your local town hall *within the next 14 days.*

COMMUNITY CHARGE DECLARATION FORM

I would like to register my pet on the Community Charge (Poll Tax) list.

NAME:

ADDRESS:

POSTCODE:

BREED:

SPECIES:

SEX:

WEIGHT (Kg):

(If you have more than one pet, please contact the finance department at your local town hall and ask for form 1/4/90/AFD (Multiple Pet Entries declaration).

CENTRAL CENSUS RECORDS DEPARTMENT

The Buildings, 14/27 Stagmorton Square, London W1 TL4
Telephone: 01-490 0688 or 071-490 0688 Ext 477

REF 178/8GH/12

Date as postmark

Dear Madam

Recent upgrading of archival material to computer storage has brought to light a number of minor errors made some years ago in the proper registration of certain infants' given names. It is therefore our duty to inform you that, in law, your correct and registered name is presently **SUSAN DEBORAH LYNNETTE WHORTON**.

You will, of course, realise that all documents and holdings in your present, incorrect name are legally invalid in this light. Would you therefore take all appropriate steps to inform your bank, building society and credit card companies, as well as government bodies such as the Community Charge Register and DVLC Swansea, of your correct and legal name.

If you wish to amend your name lawfully, you should put your request in writing to the above address, but please be aware that the full legal process can take up to two years to complete and may involve personal expense of a substantial nature.

Yours faithfully

Executive Officer

CENTRAL CENSUS RECORDS DEPARTMENT

The Buildings, 14/27 Stagmorton Square, London W1 TL4
Telephone: 01-490 0688 or 071-490 0688 Ext 477

REF 143/8GH/12

Date as postmark

Dear Sir

Recent upgrading of archival material to computer storage has brought to light a number of minor errors made some years ago in the proper registration of certain infants' given names. It is therefore our duty to inform you that, in law, your correct and registered name is presently **BRUCE MICHAEL PHILLIP FREDERICKS**.

You will, of course, realise that all documents and holdings in your present, incorrect name are legally invalid in this light. Would you therefore take all appropriate steps to inform your bank, building society and credit card companies, as well as government bodies such as the Community Charge Register and DVLC Swansea, of your correct and legal name.

If you wish to amend your name lawfully, you should put your request in writing to the above address, but please be aware that the full legal process can take up to two years to complete and may involve personal expense of a substantial nature.

Yours faithfully

Executive Officer

VETERINARY ADVICE ASSOCIATION

124 Glastonbury Square
Fosdyke Street
London WC2 TL4.

Telephone: 01-490 0688
or 071-490 0688

Established 1897

COLOSTO-GENITAL ANTHRAX DISEASE - CRISIS BULLETIN # 4

Dear Sir or Madam

We are contacting residents in this area to bring to their attention a recent outbreak of the contagious animal disease 'Colosto-Genital Anthrax'.

Approximately 20% of household pets in this area have so far been affected. This particular strain is believed to have been brought into the country by the Spanish Flying Anthrax Beetle (*Dilantipus iberius*), a species indigenous to Northern Spain and closely resembling the Common Ladybird (*Paracolia paracolia*).

It is very important to isolate any pets found to be infected by the disease and to seek veterinary advice at the earliest possible opportunity.

'Colosto-Genital Anthrax' can be identified by small red blotches present in the pubic region of domestic pets, and by the tendency of infected animals to roll onto their backs for no apparent reason. (The early stages of the disease affect the central nervous system, triggering short spasms.)

A simple test can be carried out at home, which will confirm whether or not your pet has been infected. Mix a sample of its urine with pasteurised milk and leave in a warm place for two hours. Any anthrax viroid culture will react with the lactic acid contained within the milk, turning it a pale green colour.

If a colour change is noticed, you are advised to contact a veterinary surgeon. The disease can sometimes be treated if its presence is detected early enough.

Thank you for your co-operation.

CHIEF VETERINARY VENEREOLOGIST

EUROPEAN ECONOMIC COMMUNITY
BUREAU OF ADMINISTRATIVE AFFAIRS

2541 Rue Plagier
Bruxelles 21467
Belgique

AMI Buildings
St Adrian's Lane
London W1 TT4
Telephone: 01-490 0688 or
071-490 0688

Dear Sir/Madam

As of 1992, the estimated population of the total
European Economic Community will be in excess of
320,000,000.

For purposes of administrative functions carried out
by the community, with this level of population it is
no longer efficient or practical to continue to file
and reference individuals on a surname and initial
basis.

From 1 January 1992, for administrative purposes,
therefore, all given names will be completely replaced
by a simple number reference which you should memorise
and use on all official documentation instead of your
name or signature. However, the system is scheduled to
be phased in immediately so that it can be completed
before the 1992 deadline, and you should take the
following steps without delay.

This number will replace your signature on all bank
cheques, in accordance with Eurobanking reference
T4:871/936/4KLI - and you should *act now* to inform
your bank of this change.

This number will also act as a full postal address, to
replace the cumbersome present system of postcodes and
you should inform all correspondents of this change,
which will come into effect within the next fortnight.

YOUR PERSONAL ADMINISTRATIVE NUMBER UNIT SUBSCRIPTION
(or 'Euronumber') will be:
GB/E471/822/713/3348K/21L

REMEMBER Using your Euronumber will ensure that
administrative costs within the EEC are kept to an
acceptable level and will facilitate the quicker
resolution of all your private and business matters.

*N.B. Keep this letter in a safe place for reference
purposes!*

INDEPENDENT DOCUMENTARY PRODUCTIONS

Riverside Studios, Loxley Park Street,
Camden, London NW1 TT4.
Telephone: 01-490 0688 or 071-490 0688
Extension 67

Date as postmark

Dear

Thank you for your completed application form and letter, volunteering to be featured in the forthcoming major television documentary, *The Reproduction Game*.

You will be delighted to learn that, from over 8,000 applications, you are among the final thirty couples shortlisted to perform on the show.

As you are aware, if you are selected, you will be asked to perform the act of coitus before a live studio audience and then join in a debate during the second half of the show. Of course, as this is a serious and respectable documentary, we are aiming to present the most straightforward consummation of the act, i.e. utilising the missionary postion, and nothing acrobatic, strenuous or unusual will be expected of you!

To take matters one step further, we propose to screen test all shortlisted couples. Your screen test is provisionally scheduled for _____am/pm on _____.

Please telephone this office at least seventy-two hours before this time, if this appointment is not convenient.

In order for us to test your ability to relax before a live audience, we'll be bringing along a 'sample audience' of ten members of the public who will be rating you for 'Charm', 'Style' and 'Likeability'.

Thank you again for volunteering to be a part of this ground-breaking event in adult television programming, and may I take this opportunity to wish you the very best of luck in your forthcoming screen test!

Yours sincerely

RESEARCHER

APOLLONIA MANNEQUINS LTD

4 Girnby Mews, off Wardour Street, London W1 TL4N.
Telephone: 01-490 0688 or 071-490 0688

Date as postmark

Dear Sir

Re: KNEELING GEISHA DOLL Mk.III

We are writing to all purchasers of the above model, warning them of two errors in the instruction manual supplied.

These have occurred during the translation of the operating instructions from Japanese to English, and, whilst not serious, might reduce the satisfaction derived from use.

Page 2 - Under 'INFLATION', second paragraph should read:
If doll is intended for use for longer than seven minutes, pressure should be increased by 7 p.s.i.

Page 3 - Under 'CLEANING INSTRUCTIONS', first paragraph should read:
All orifices should be wiped down with a damp sponge immediately after use. Do not use proprietary cleaning liquids.

We are currently having the manual reprinted and will be forwarding a revised edition to you shortly, along with our new colour catalogue and price list.

Thank you for your regular custom.

Yours faithfully

Duende
2, Portmerion Street
London SW14 TL4

Telephone: 01-490 0688
or 071-490 0688

Date as postmark

Dear Sir

I am writing to you in connection with my research for the forthcoming book, *Hitler - The Missing Generations*.

According to records in the Bunderkretz Centrische in Vienna, you are a great nephew (twice removed) of Alois Gustav Hitler, Adolf Hitler's natural father. If these records are accurate, this would make you his distant cousin.

I would be interested to know if you ever met Herr Hitler and, if so, whether you have any personal or amusing anecdotes or photographs which I might use for publication. You would of course receive full credit for any assistance you might provide.

I would also be interested in meeting you at a point in the near future to go through some old photo albums in my possession. It is possible that you might be able to put names to some of the faces of both family members and founding members of the Nazi Party.

I will ring you next week to arrange a convenient time for us to meet.

In closing, could you also let me know whether or not you would be prepared to go on radio or television to speak about your family ties, by way of publicity for the book.

Yours faithfully

Robbie Trainton   FREELANCE WRITER

CZECHOSLOVAKIAN CHAMBER OF COMMERCE

14/27 Synbrooke Place,
Synbrooke Street,
London WC1 TL4.
Telephone: 01-490 0688 or 071-490 0688

Dear Sir or Madam

We are most delightful to announce you as much worthy winner in great 'Joyous Czechoslovakia' media competition. Only you with corrected answers to splendid Czechoslovakian history questions. You much clever and study hard to triumph? Yes?

As victorious contestant we salute you and pleasure to us in announce the number one best top prize offer to you!

You win the mechanic marvel of Czechoslovakian engineering greatness. The SKODA 130LS. Yes! A new SKODA 130LS is delivered bang slap to your door Saturday next at 10.30 morning time.

But this no ordinary SKODA 130LS. No boy!

Hey presto! Many extras we fit to make prize special. Look see what additions we make.

- Gold paint and snazzy roof with vinyl top!
- Whitewall tyres just like Yankee speed demon automobiles!
- Wipers windscreen slow AND rapide!
- Springs in front and rear-back seating to float your passage!
- LW/MW radio set for toe-tapping sounds on move!
- Front AND back rubber mats so no spoiling carpets!
- Brightly fog lights so no danger in Britain vegetable-souper!
- Fully locking boot at back so secure your breakdown tooling!

Your neighbours not even believing their own oculars when they see much admired and new SKODA 130LS delivered to your home next week! Huh! Keeping up with the Dzrovnikovz family or what! Photography arranged by us as well, so you end up smile in locality newspapers. People will stop you for signature in street! You be local star much like Frank Sinatra!

With very best of wishes

G. Ostrava
External Affairs

OFFICE TELEPHONE MESSAGE PAD

TO: _____

FROM: _____

TIME: _____

MESSAGE TAKEN BY: _____

The clinic called. They say they're totally baffled because it's a strain found only in farm animals. Could you call them back urgently on 01-490 0688 or 071-490 0688 and then lock yourself away from decent people –

OFFICE TELEPHONE MESSAGE PAD

TO: _____

FROM: _____

TIME: _____

MESSAGE TAKEN BY: _____

The abortion clinic called. They say they're sorry, but they removed your appendix by mistake and you'll have to go back next week. Call them on 01.490.0688 or 071.490.0688 for an appointment.

OFFICE TELEPHONE MESSAGE PAD

TO: _____

FROM: _____

TIME: _____

MESSAGE TAKEN BY: _____

A Mrs. Dearn called. She said to leave her husband alone you wanton slut or she'll pull your dyed hair out by the roots.

OFFICE TELEPHONE MESSAGE PAD

TO: _____

FROM: _____

TIME: _____

MESSAGE TAKEN BY: _____

'PENTHOUSE' PHONED. THEY SAY THE TEST SHOTS LOOK PROMISING AND THEY'LL CALL BACK. IF YOU WANT TO RING THEM, THE NUMBER'S 01-490 0688 or 071-490 0688

Our Ref: PHML22095K534/001/PH

Your ref: ENG/AGP/25

Dear

This is to confirm the receipt of your application form to open an account with us, with a guarantee from you of a weekly order of at least 50 cylinders of welding gas.

Your account number is: PHML22095K34. We would be grateful if you could keep a record of this, and quote it when you make an order.

Your first order, comprising 1.500 46.5kg 5ft cylinders of propane gas, will be delivered to your address within seventy-two hours, on our reference number: 32588AF. An invoice for the cylinder rental and cost of the gas will be posted to you forthwith.

We ask that you adhere to the following safety regulations necessary when dealing with a highly flammable gas such as propane.

1. Check each cylinder daily for leakage of gas. If leakage occurs, tighten the gland nut by the valve at the top of the cylinder. If the leakage continues, phone the fire brigade immediately, and evacuate the area within a hundred-yard radius of the cylinders.

2. All cylinders must be used within one week of delivery to avoid de-stabilising or implosion of the cylinders. Unfortunately, although we are usually happy to collect full or partially used propane cylinders before the week is up, we have a slight dispute with our fillers and loaders at present, and are unable to quote a collection date. It is therefore preferable that you phone either the police or our emergency control number (01-490 0688 or 071-490 0688, Extension 455) only in the extreme circumstance of your not being able to use all cylinders. We do have a charge for this service of £5.00 per cylinder, as quoted in Note 5 of the application form.

3. The cylinders must be stored outside and must not be exposed to any naked flame, oven heat or electrical switching activity such as the activating of lights or mains-powered plant. Please do not wear steel-capped boots near these cylinders as the friction can cause ignition. People who wear glasses or contact lenses should be well aware of the danger to their eyes when dealing with this hazardous gas.

4. Before the valve is opened, you must make sure that you have the other two gases necessary for welding with propane: oxygen and dissolved acetylene. Failure to use these gases will result in fire.

Thank you for your order.

In the assurance of our most courteous attention at all times.

Yours faithfully

Gas Order Clerk
Customer Services Department

AUNTY DEBBIE'S HANDY HOUSEHOLD HINTS

Issued free by *WOMAN* & *KITCHEN* Magazine

MAKING HOUSEHOLD OBJECTS LAST LONGER

LIGHT BULBS: To make light bulbs last longer, freeze them for about two hours and then plunge them into boiling water. This will condense the gas, giving up to 20% longer life.

BRILLO PADS: Rubbing old scouring pads in a mixture of talcum powder and lemon juice will revitalise the soap within them.

BATTERIES: Extend the life of batteries by keeping them in a solution of cold tea overnight before use.

ELASTIC BANDS: Perished elastic bands can be renewed by warming them in citric acid (lemon or orange juice).

WASHING UP LIQUID: Make this go further by diluting it, 4 parts washing up liquid to 1 part methylated spirits; you'll find it even lathers better than before.

SHAMPOO: Adding a teaspoon of sunflower oil to shampoo will make it last longer and give hair a natural, healthy shine.

CANDLES: Candles will burn more slowly if a knob of butter is allowed to soak into the wicks before they are lit.

BIROS: To make the ink in your pen last longer, rub the nib over a piece of fresh greaseproof paper before writing.

BISCUITS: To prevent delicious biscuits from going soft and stale, wrap them in socks together with a teaspoon of cold mashed potato and place in the bottom drawer of the oven until it's time to eat them!

HOME LAUNDRY

IRONING: For sharper creases, iron through a handkerchief soaked in milk. You'll notice the difference straight away.

TUMBLE DRIERS: A cup of sugar added to the load gives the wash a natural, fresh smell.

WASHING MACHINES: Sprinkling table salt over woollen items will help lift dirt

---

CARING FOR KITCHEN UTENSILS

SCISSORS: Sharpen your own scissors by cutting several strips off a piece of coarse sandpaper.

FOOD PROCESSORS: Blending several salted egg yolks once every month will keep the cutting edges clean and sharp.

NON-STICK PANS: All 'non-stick' surfaces wear out after a while. However, a way to renew them until they are replaced is to boil until dry a mixture of cooking oil and instant coffee.

KNIVES: After use, stick the blades in a potato. You'll be surprised at the difference this will make.

EGG WHISKS: If these tend to stick, rub a piece of orange rind on the gear mechanism.

WEIGHT CONVERSION CHART

Oz/fluid oz.	grammes/ml
1	36
2	72
3	108
4	144
5 (1/4 pint)	180
6	216
7	252
8	288
9	324
10 (1/2 pint)	360

---

that is ingrained into the fibres.

FADED LINEN: Old pillowcases, sheets and tablecloths can be revitalised if they're soaked overnight in a sink filled with hot water and rhubarb.

SCORCH MARKS: Light scorch marks can be removed by rubbing treacle or golden syrup into them before washing.

Dear Readers

Thank you for writing in with an SAE to request my Handy Household Hints leaflet. I know many of you have been cutting my hints out of *Woman & Kitchen* over the past few months and I've had a lot of letters asking if they can be reprinted in a convenient single sheet. Well, here it is.

Keep it in the kitchen and you'll be amazed at how much time (and money) you can save just by following some of these simple tips.

Happy housekeeping!

Aunty Debbie

Published by *Woman & Kitchen* magazine, 34 Sylvia Street, London WC4N TL4.

Telephone: 01-490 0688 or 071-490 0688

CLEANING TIPS

SHOES: If you've run out of shoe polish, a beef stock cube mixed with hand cream makes a good substitute.

GLASS: Egg whites will leave every window clear and repel condensation. Apply with a chamois leather.

PARQUET FLOORING: Use a mixture of mustard powder and TCP (1:5 by weight) to restore the natural colour of wood veneer.

SILVER: A Brillo pad soaked in vinegar will restore the sparkle to heavily tarnished items.

WROUGHT IRON: A coating of natural yoghurt diluted by white spirit will repel rust and make gates shine. Repeat every two to three months.

RADIATORS: Avoid heat discolouration by wiping a damp tea bag over the paintwork.

BRASS: Apply a coating of advocaat, leave for an hour and then rinse off.

SUEDE: Shiny patches of suede can be removed by soaking in Coca-Cola and rubbing gently with sandpaper.

PIANO KEYS: Discoloured ivory keys may be restored by applying a small amount of tinned rice pudding on a soft cloth and gently wiping.

PINE: Rubbing cheese slowly over its surface will restore the grain in pine furniture.

LEATHER: You can protect and prolong the life of leather furniture and clothing by applying a thin layer of melted candle wax to the surface area. Leave to harden overnight and then simply peel off the excess wax!

PURE WOOL: To prevent shrinking in the wash, coat with a layer of cottage cheese, leave overnight and then place garment in wash *without* removing the cheese.

PAPER: To prevent treasured books from yellowing and becoming brittle, immerse them in a solution of vinegar and Benilyn (14 parts vinegar to 1 part Benilyn).

PHOTOGRAPHS: You can stop irreplaceable photos from fading by wrapping them in cooking foil and then baking them in a low oven for three hours (black and white) or six hours (colour).

GAS/ELECTRIC OVEN CONVERSION CHART

Electric	Gas Mark
110°C	1
130°C	2
140°C	3
150°C	4
160°C	5
180°C	6
190°C	7
200°C	8
220°C	9
230°C	10

CORRECT IRONING TEMPERATURES

MATERIAL	MAXIMUM TEMP.
Acetate, acrylic, nylon	170°C (338°F)
Polyester/cotton mixes, wool	210°C (410°F)
Cotton, linen, viscose	260°C (500°F)

LENGTH CONVERSION CHART

Imperial	Metric
1 inch	2.77 cms
1 foot	33.33 cms
1 yard	100.0 cms (1 metre)

TAXATION TOM'S
SECRET AGENT
CLUB

Dear Children

Are you interested in the mysterious world of spies and secret agents?

Well, if you are, **you can help me out on an important mission!** If you accept, you must remember one thing - it's a secret that only children can know about. No adults must be told a thing or else the whole plan will be in danger.

Are you interested? Yes? Well, let me tell you about this mission and how you can help!

I work for a big organisation called the Inland Revenue. It's not as exciting as the place that James Bond works for, but the work we do is still very 'hush-hush'. We collect 'taxes' from parents who go to work; this money then goes towards manufacturing childrens' toys and games.

Without this money there would be no childrens' toys at all - so you can see how important it is that we collect it! Sadly, though, we know that some parents have extra jobs in their spare time which they don't pay taxes on. This makes us angry because if they don't pay up, children will have to go without toys.

You can help us by letting us know if your parents have more than one job. For example, they might work in a pub in the evenings, or they might have a cleaning job somewhere. Whatever it is, we want to hear about it!

But remember, this must be kept a secret! All you have to do is call us at your local tax office (we're in the *Yellow Pages*) or at our central top secret headquarters on 01-490 0688 or 071-490 0688 and give us the details. It's probably best to phone when your parents are out - otherwise they might get suspicious!

We won't be annoyed with your parents - they've probably just forgotten to tell us about their other job - all we want is to make sure that children everywhere are happy and have plenty of toys to play with.

Thanks for all your help!

Remember that mum's the word - but don't tell yours about it!

Good luck

TAXATION TOM

THE COMPLETE REVENGE KIT RESTAURANT SPECIALITE DU JOUR

INSTRUCTIONS FOR USE:
If you're receiving particularly bad service in a restaurant from your waiter, call him over. Fold up one of the notes below and ask him to give it to a particular woman in the restaurant - but not to say which table it came from . . .

I may be just a lowly waiter with no car, no money in the bank and no prospects, but I adore you with all my heart and would love to put my hand up your skirt.

Guiseppe XXXXX

My l'amour petite,

I have mingled my love essence with your dish!

The waiter with the twinkling eyes

I noticed you've been smiling at me all evening as I wend my way between the tables, and I think I can guess what's on your mind!

I'm thinking the same thing too, so meet me round the back by the dustbins after closing time if you want a really stiff seeing-to.
XXXX

Madam

The gourmet guide inspectors are due to visit us today and we do not wish them to think that riff-raff such as yourself are an accurate representation of our regular clientele.

Would you therefore oblige us by removing yourself from our premises forthwith, before we eject you.

The management

Waiters depend for their livelihood on tips. But you look like a mean old cow, so I'm warning you now: if you don't leave me a bloody big tip, I'm going to trip you up on the way out - and make it look like an accident.

Your friendly waiter

HEAVY METAL MONTHLY

Incorporating THRASH METAL NEWS

Address for all editorial correspondence:
14C Clarkhamwell Street, London EC12 TL7.
Telephone: 01-490 0688 or 071-490 0688

Dear HEAVY METAL FREAK!

We're proud to announce that you're one of the three winners of our fantastic 'Win A Night Out With SATAN'S SLAYERS' competition!

And what a night out it's going to be! MAAAADNEEESSSSSSSSS!

Just look at what you can expect! The fun begins at 6.00 next Saturday night when the band's converted HEARSE will pick you and a friend up at your home address. Just imagine the look on your neighbours' faces (not to mention yer mum's!) when vocalist RICHIE ST CADAVER, in his OUTRAGEOUS stage costume complete with skull cod-piece and double-bladed AXE, walks up to your front door and escorts you to the car.

You'll then be blindfolded as it weaves its way on a TRAGICAL MYSTERY TOUR into the unknown. At the SECRET destination you'll meet the rest of the band - in the living (or as near as they can get !!!) FLESH!

Then it's PARTY TIME! PAAAAAARRRRRRTTYY! The theme is the title of their latest album, 'KILL ME BEFORE TEA TIME' and some of their antics that night will make even ALICE COOPER look TAME!!!

The party's supposed to end around midnight, but if past events are anything to go by, be prepared for thirty-six hours WITHOUT SLEEP!

We promise you a night you'll never forget. When the band gets going, they STOP AT NOTHING in the pursuit of a GOOD TIME! Morals, good taste, common sense, human endurance, the law - they all go out of the window (which the SLAYERS have probably SMASHED as well!!!).

Tell your mother not to wait up. Better still, tell her to inform the Bureau for Missing Persons - only kidding!!!

Bet you can't wait!

See you Saturday and, as the band says, you'll have so much fun, you'll DIE laughing!!!!

Now, what are you waiting for? Go out and PAAAAARRRRRRRTTYYYYY!!!!!

Editor

THE LONDON INSTITUTE OF HOME LEARNING

2nd Floor, Oxbridge Road, London SW10 TL4.　　　　Telephone: 01-490 0688 or 071-490 0688

Date as postmark

Dear Sir

Thank you for your completed application form and course fees. We are pleased to announce that you have now been enrolled at the London Institute of Home Learning on our 'Pathology by Post' course which begins next week.

With the growing interest in forensic science, pathology is proving to be a popular career choice for the 1990s. Our 'Pathology by Post' course and the qualifications it gives are officially recognised by the Home Office, who act as consultants.

Although this is a recent addition to our wide range of correspondence courses, over seventy successful graduating students have already secured well-paid positions as pathologists both here and abroad.

Since your initial enquiry there has been a minor amendment to the course structure. The new prospectus is set out below.

Yours sincerely

<u>Director of Studies</u>

PATHOLOGY BY POST
1990 - 91 Prospectus
Course length: 80 weeks

'Pathology by Post' is the only correspondence course to teach every aspect of forensic science. The drawback of most correspondence courses is that practical experience is difficult or extremely limited. However, the structure of 'Pathology by Post' places the emphasis firmly on 'hands-on' experience and enables students to learn both practical and theoretical aspects of this subject.

A fresh cadaver will be delivered to your door each week* in a vacuum-sealed body bag, accompanied by a set of comprehensive course notes. These will give details of the victim, circumstances of the case and advice as to how to perform the post mortem. Initially the cause of death will be relatively easy to identify; however, this will become more difficult as the course progresses.

By about Week 60 students should be able to recognise different bullets by their characteristic exit wounds and to identify eight types of poison by examining the contents of a victim's colon and rectum.

Throughout the course, infamous murders are recreated and used as 'case histories' for students. In each case the body is supplied in exactly the same condition in which it was discovered. For example, in the case of Jack the Ripper's fourth victim, the body will be supplied with the heart removed, face stripped of skin and entrails slung over the left shoulder.

The final ten weeks of the course are taken up by practising surgical procedures and revising the technicalities of brain death, blood loss and asphyxiation.

All our tutors are in regular communication with students for the duration of the course and will make personal visits every six weeks to check on progress.

(Course fees do not include surgical instruments. These may be purchsed separately from any medical equipment supplier.)

IMPORTANT: Please remember to advise us at least two weeks in advance when you are going on holiday so that we may postpone delivery of specimens.

* The special 'Pathology by Post' crash course (involving three bodies per week, but requiring a large freezer) has now been discontinued.

TO THE PHARMACIST

1. Please accept this coupon in exchange for TYMIL Laboratories' 'Stonkothyl' or 'Boneryl' sample packs, as agreed under our promotional contract.

2. This coupon is invalid with any other offer or promotion on all TYMIL Laboratories products.

2. This coupon is invalid with any other offer or promotion on all TYMIL Laboratories products.

TO THE RETAILER

1. This coupon is only redeemable in exchange for one 1lb packet of Schweter's Jumbo-sized Frankfurters - plus 3p commission charge - and cannot be used in conjunction with any other product, offer or promotion.

2. This coupon is only valid on special 'Whanger' packets delivered by our sales representative in conjunction with this promotion.

3. This offer becomes void when your stock of promotional packs has been used - and this coupon may *not* be redeemed against regular 'Whanger' packs.

4. Only one coupon may be redeemed per customer.

EUROPEAN ECONOMIC COMMUNITY
BUREAU OF ADMINISTRATION AND PLANNING

2541 Rue Plagier
Bruxelles 24167
Belgique

AMI Buildings
St Adrian's Lane
London W1 TT4
Telephone: 01-490 0688 or
071-490 0688

Attention: Householder

Monsieur le Clique, the funny Eurotime clock, is here to herald an exciting new change in the way we tell the time prior to 1992!

As you know by now, in 1992 we shall all be a single community, with a single business market, and to facilitate the most productive and efficient use of working hours within the EEC, plans are now well under way to implement the decimalisation of time.

The old imperial system of 60 seconds to a minute, 24 hours to a day and 7 days to an imperial week is riddled with inconsistencies and is naturally therefore confusing and in urgent need of reform.

The new system, to come into effect on 1 January 1992, is to be called 'Eurotime' and will offer a vastly simplified 'decimalised' time programme, with 10 Euroseconds to the Eurominute, 100 Eurominutes to the Eurohour, 10 Eurohours to one Euroday and 10 Eurodays to one Euroweek. Further to this, there will be 10 Euroweeks to one Euromonth and 10 Euromonths to one Euroyear. Decades will remain unchanged.

As the new Euroyear will be composed of 10 as opposed to 12 months, it is proposed that they be completely renamed in honour of the longest serving members of the European Parliament.

While converting to the new time system, you will easily be able to reckon the Eurotime equivalent of any imperial time simply by multiplying the number by 12.374 and then dividing the result by 4.42 and subtracting 7.

A full brochure and handy reckoning table, featuring Monsieur le Clique, will be sent to your property closer to the time of conversion. In the meantime, if your joint income is below £10,000 per annum, you may qualify for a grant to convert your household to Eurotime, and should apply now, care of your local MEP.

WASTE-RITE REFUSE COLLECTION LTD

National Offices: 4 Cinderbridge Industrial Estate, Cinderbridge Road, Battersea, London SE1 TL4.
Telephone: 01- 490 0688 or 071- 490 0688

Date as Postmark

Dear Householder

You have probably read in your local paper that Waste-Rite Ltd has now been appointed as official private Refuse Collectors for this borough.

We begin our contract next month. However, to make our service more efficient and economical, the following changes will need to take place:

1. It is no longer economically viable to collect refuse on a weekly basis. Your standard plastic household dustbin will be replaced free of charge with a large steel commercial refuse receptacle. One will be allocated to each household and collections will be made once a month. At only 6' tall and 4' in diameter, these bins can be made to look attractive and quite discreet if painted to match the exterior decor of your house.

2. To enable efficient recycling of household waste, the following types of non-bio-degradable refuse must be wrapped in black plastic sacks and labelled accordingly:
— plastic containers
— glassware
— contraceptives and other rubber products
— newspapers and magazines

3. To alleviate traffic congestion, refuse collections will take place between the hours of 2 and 5 am. To reduce noise from our Refuse Collection Vehicles, residents are advised to keep their windows firmly closed.

4. Refuse Collection Operatives will no longer embarrass individual residents by requesting a Christmas tip. Instead, a 'Seasonal Gratuity Payment' will be added to the local Community Charge and automatically paid to each Operative at the end of the year.

We look forward to serving you and improving the standards of Refuse Collection in your borough. Our Customer Liaison Department is on hand during office hours to deal with any queries regarding our service.

Yours sincerely

Local Operations Manager

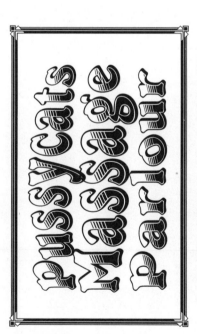

Pussycats
4 Gimby Mews
Off Wardour Street
London W1 TL4N

Telephone:
01-490 0688
or 071-490 0688

SATISFACTION AT A STROKE!

Dear Sir,

I am writing to remind you that your annual membership for 'Pussycats' expires in thirty days.

When you consider the excellent services provided by the parlour, including the Swedish birch twig treatment and the two-girl touch therapy, as well as the jacuzzi/video room and our brand new Palais de Rubber room, I am sure you will not hesitate to renew your membership forthwith.

If you are thinking of letting your membership lapse, I should remind you that, during the forthcoming year, we will be adding a wealth of exciting new features to the club, including Nurse Felicity's blanket baths (Mon to Thurs), 'Horsie Races' and the semolina tactile therapy trough – attractions I am sure you won't want to miss out on!

Please drop us a line confirming that you wish to remain a member and notify your bank to pay the direct debit registered in the name of 'Portland's Businessmen's Club'.

See you at 'Pussycats' again soon!

I'm pregnant, you bastard!

Ring me at my Mums.

The numbers
01-490 0688
(071-490 0688)

BUCKINGHAM PALACE

Dear

Her Majesty The Queen has asked me to inform you that she was most interested to hear of your vasectomy and wishes you a speedy recovery.

Yours

Royal Equerry

BUCKINGHAM PALACE

Dear

I am commanded to inform you that His Royal Highness The Prince Philip was most interested to hear that you own some waterfowl and would be pleased to come round and shoot them at a time to be mutually agreed.

Yours

Royal Equerry

BUCKINGHAM PALACE

Dear

Further to your letter, I regret to inform you that Her Royal Highness The Duchess of York (who should properly be addressed thus at all times and not as 'Fergie', such as your letter began) has no old ballgowns or dresses which she can let you have.

She asks me to inform you that many excellent department stores in London now stock outsized clothing for bigger women and that you should have no problems finding glamorous clothes in the size you require.
Yours

Royal Equerry

BUCKINGHAM PALACE

Dear

Her Majesty The Queen has asked me to inform you that she cannot offer you a knighthood in exchange for financial remuneration.

Might I suggest you try the local branch of your Conservative Party?

Yours

Royal Equerry

Spartacus Gay Dating Bureau

Registered Offices:
12b Gregoran Mews, Victoria, London SW1 TL4.
Telephone: 01-490 0688 or 071-490 0688

Dear

Thank you for your completed membership form and fee.

Here at Spartacus we operate a very close personal service on your behalf. We have already entered you on our computer and this initial letter gives details of three of our most compatible members.

They're listed below and each one is identified by a reference number. Please reply to our offices, quoting the number of the contact(s) which interest you and we will put them in touch.

> **TRACY** (L587T) is in her early twenties and is a college student completing a course in Women's Studies. She hopes to form a video documentary unit for ethnic women in inner city areas 'to express their plight and re-affirm their gendo-ethnicity'. Tracy describes herself as 'independent, tough and forthright - but with a sense of humour'. Hobbies include CND, cycling, solar energy and Greenpeace. She is a vegetarian.

> **CATHY** (T158). Cathy is employed by a local council and is working towards a City and Guilds Certificate in 'Fencing and Bricklaying'. She lives with her pet cats, and hobbies include cycling, photography, DIY and 'Protesting against Thatcher's fascist junta'. Cathy, in her own words, is 'physically fit, adventurous and good fun to be with'.

> **HILARY** (W178). Although Hilary, twenty-eight, describes herself as 'a bit of a mess, physically', she believes she has a lot to offer the right person. Her hobbies include campaigning for nuclear disarmament, cinema, making her own clothes and cycling holidays abroad. Hilary is unemployed at the moment and regards herself as just another of 'Thatcher's millions'. Prior to this she worked in an outsize clothing store.

Your phone number has, of course, now been included on the 'Gay Hotline', our free listing service distributed to all subscribers.

We wish you every success in finding the partner of your dreams. Do not hesitate to contact us at any time.

You will be receiving updated lists of contacts on a regular basis, and notification of subscription renewal will be sent well in advance.

In sisterhood

Branches throughout the UK

Spartacus Gay Dating Bureau

Registered Offices:
12b Gregoran Mews, Victoria, London SW1 TL4.
Telephone: 01-490 0688 or 071-490 0688

Dear

Thank you for your completed membership form and fee.

Here at Spartacus we operate a very close personal service on your behalf. We have already entered you on our computer and this initial letter gives details of three of our most compatible members.

They're listed below and each one is identified by a reference number. Please reply to our offices, quoting the number of the contact(s) which interest you and we will put them in touch.

> **GRANT** (B567W) describes himself as 'cuddly, introverted and warm-hearted'. He is in his early thirties and has built himself a highly successful career in textiles. He owns his own home. Non-smoker. Lists his interests as 'squash, cycling, reading, classical music and origami'.

> **BARTHOLEMEW** (Z153). 'Bartie' - as he likes to be known - is in his late twenties. He describes himself as affectionate and home-loving. He has worked abroad for the past eight years and has recently returned to 'settle down with that special someone'. A non-smoker, Bartie breeds toy poodles when he is not working, and greatly enjoys continental films and classical music. He has a prize collection of model soldiers, and often exhibits at shows.

> **KEVIN** (G318Q) is in his mid-twenties and is a fitness fanatic which, he says 'keeps him in good stead on the construction site'. Kevin describes himself as 'tender, loyal and caring, but with a cheeky sense of humour'. A non-smoker, his interests include listening to all types of music, squash, weight-training and sailing remote-controlled boats.

Your phone number has, of course, now been included on the 'Gay Hotline', our free listing service distributed to all subscribers.

We wish you every success in finding the partner of your dreams. Do not hesitate to contact us at any time.

You will be receiving updated lists of contacts on a regular basis, and notification of subscription renewal will be sent well in advance.

Fraternally yours

Branches throughout the UK

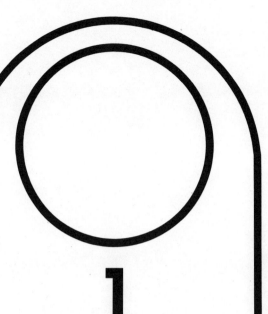

1

EXTRA PINT PLEASE

P.S. My husband's gone to work and I'm wearing a skimpy black negligée that leaves nothing to the imagination.

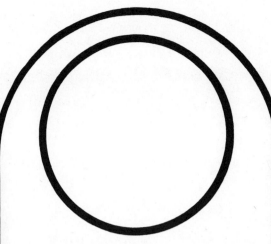

PISS OFF MILKMAN

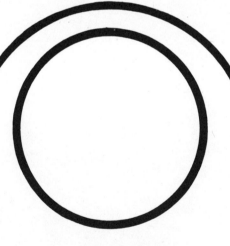

A GOOD SEEING-TO PLEASE

(and an extra gold top)

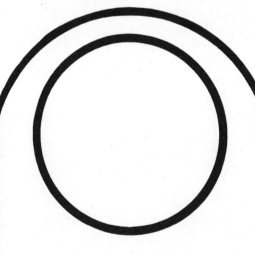

My husband's found out! He'll kill you if he sees you!

Date as postmark

Dear Commuter

We are writing to all season ticket holders to advise them of the Council's recent decision to allow nuclear waste to be transported through this area by rail.

Having had several meetings with the Council and the Government Health and Safety Executive, we are satisfied that the necessary safety precautions will be observed once transportation of the waste commences next month.

Although 'waste-only' trains were originally planned, the non-availability of special rolling stock means that the nuclear waste will now be carried aboard regular commuter trains to London. It will be packed within lead-lined containers mounted beneath the first four carriages of each train.

We have been assured that the radiation emitted by the waste is minimal, but to allay the public's fears, geiger counters will be fitted in each carriage.

Although drivers and guards will be wearing radiation suits we have been informed that this is purely a precaution and no reflection whatsoever on the safety of the nuclear cargo.

In order to fit these containers, trains will have to be temporarily withdrawn from service and there may be a number of cancellations on services throughout the region. However, in order to minimise disruption, they will be converted gradually over a one-month period.

Yours sincerely

Regional Liaison Manager

DEPARTMENT OF NATIONALISATION

34 Gillburton Street
London W9 RL3.

Telephone: 01-490 0688
or 071-490 0688 Ext 616

Date:

Our ref: RT/6/jf

Your ref:

Dear Sir

We are pleased to announce that following the submission of your recent marriage documentation, your application for Turkish nationality has been approved by the Turkish Consulate.

All necessary paperwork is currently being processed by the Home Office who have confirmed your new identity, under Islam, as Abdul Ben Yahaluf.

As you are aware, from receipt of this letter your current British passport becomes invalid and a new Turkish passport is being issued under separate cover.

The Inland Revenue and your employer have already been notified of your new status as a Turkish citizen in order to prepare your final PAYE and National Insurance coding accordingly.

The Turkish Consulate will be happy to advise you of your new rights and benefits as a Turkish national.

With good wishes to you and your new bride.

Yours sincerely

Administration Officer

MORAL DILEMMA

THE *ADULT* TALK SHOW

Independent Productions Co Ltd,
Riverside Studios,
Loxley Park Road,
Camden,
London NW1 TT4.
Telephone: 01-490 0688 or
071-490 0688 Ext 71

Dear Sir

We are pleased to announce that you've been selected as a panellist taking part in our live debate next Friday evening.

We were very impressed with your letter and your arguments for making the laws concerning sexual relationships with animals more lenient. There's not too many people willing to talk about this live in front of 8 million viewers, as you can guess.

From your experiences listed, it's clear that this is a subject which you feel passionately about. Right or wrong, it's not for us to judge - that's what the studio audience does!

And to help the audience decide, we're pleased to have some noteworthy guests taking part. These include an eminent psychiatrist, a chief constable, the royal veterinarian and a spokesman from the RSPCA.

A courtesy car will pick you up from home at 8.30 pm on Friday. At the studio there'll be time for a bite and a chance to meet Marion Davis, the presenter, before the show goes out live at 11.00. A car will then take you home - expect to be back about 12.30.

Look forward to seeing you then,

Research Assistant

THE HONG FA LO CLINIC
17/35 Quartermain Street, London WC2 TL4.
Telephone:01-490 0688 or 071-490 0688

Date as postmark

Dear

Thank you for taking up our introductory offer of a FREE home examination, as our way of introducing you to the positive benefits of acute acupuncture therapy.

Although gaining in popularity throughout the Western world, acupuncture is still something of a mystery to most people and, prior to your examination, I would like to explain to you precisely what acupuncture is, and what it does.

Acupuncture is founded on well-established 3,000-year-old Chinese medical principles, and involves the insertion of long, slender metal needles into the 'Lines of Life' or 'Central Nervous System' to relieve pain, diagnose ill-health or to help ward off invading Sand Djinns or Devil Monkeys from the 10th level.

As part of your free examination, we will be inserting a relatively small number of 'Shi-ows' or 'Needles' at equidistant positions, ranging from between your toes to your left ear (the left ear is considered the 'Sha-Ho' or 'Lodge of the Spirit' by many traditional acupuncturists). A total of 257 needles will be sufficient for the purposes of a general health check.

To examine you, the doctor will then test the health of every part of your body by applying abrupt pressure to the head of each needle in turn. The depth to which it sinks into the body determines the relative healthiness of that portion (multiplied by your age and the phase of the Chinese Lunar Cycle under which you were born).

There are many fallacies held about acupuncture, the most prevalent of which is the idea that it doesn't hurt. Of course, there is some discomfort, or actual physical pain, involved in the process, especially when - in healthy areas - needles may be driven in too far and need to be removed with pliers. We would never seek to hide this. BUT THE POSITIVE DIAGNOSTIC AND HEALING POWERS OF ACUPUNCTURE FAR OUTWEIGH THE SUFFERING INVOLVED.

Your free medical examination at home has been provisionally arranged for
_____at _____ am/pm.
Please advise the clinic if this time is not convenient to you.

Yours faithfully

Medical Administrative Officer

DEPARTMENT OF VEHICLE SAFETY

4th Floor, Feathergate Buildings,
Enthorpe Street, London WC2 TL4
Telephone: 01-490 0688
or 071-490 0688 Ext 329

Date as postmark

Dear Sir/ Madam

Re: **Your car, registration no. . . . . .**

The manufacturers have asked us to contact you to advise that the above vehicle has been recalled for emergency repairs.

From central registration information we know that yours is one of a batch of approximately 15,000 vehicles affected by a fault in the gear selector mechanism.

This is due to metal fatigue in a particular batch of castings and unless treated immediately can result in the engine slipping out of top gear into reverse at speeds of over 20 mph. This can happen completely without warning, causing the whole engine block to break from its mountings and break through the bonnet - leading to considerable damage and possible loss of control of the vehicle.

The manufacturers advise that you drive your vehicle at not more than 10 mph to the nearest main agent. On presentation of this letter the replacement gear selector will be fitted free of charge. Work can be carried out with the engine in situ, although the job will take three to four hours.

Thanking you for your co-operation in this matter.

Vehicle Recall Liaison

National Offices:
Molotov Hall, Loxley Park Street, Camden, London NW1
TT4. Telephone: 01-490 0688 or 071-490 0688 Ext 2

Date as postmark

Dear Sir/Madam

Thank you very much for your kind letter and offer of help. As you know, as an organisation dedicated to the welfare of ex-prisoners, we rely on the kind actions of volunteers like yourself.

Your name and address have now been circulated to all ex-prisoners living in your area with the information that they may call on you, any time, day or night, for advice, help - or just for a friendly chat over a cup of tea.

I am sure you understand that a lot of ex-prisoners are misunderstood and find it difficult to adapt to society on their release; especially the more violent ones who might have been locked away in solitary confinement for a considerable part of their incarceration.

It's people like you who can help to keep them on the straight and narrow, no matter what crimes and acts they might have committed in the past.

Thank you again for your kind help.

Yours sincerely

G.R.F.

Gastric Research Foundation

The Bellwood Institute, 130 Oxbridge Street, London WC3 TR1.
Telephone: 01-490 0688 or 071-490 0688 EXT 510

Date as postmark

Dear Sir/Madam

Thank you for writing to us to request further information on the GRF and volunteering to assist in our programme to determine the causes of intestinal discomfort.

It is estimated that 200,000 adults in the UK suffer from severe flatulence (*Flatus intercostus*), causing them to lead uncomfortable and embarrassing lives.

This medical condition, because of its sadly misplaced comical overtones, is misunderstood and under-researched. Our aim at the Gastric Research Foundation is to monitor and assess the many causes of flatulence in the hope that we can develop a cure to end the suffering and misery of thousands.

As a private clinic, we rely on donations and help from the public - both flatulence sufferers and non-sufferers alike. For obvious reasons our trustees like to remain anonymous but inclde several company directors, five Conservative MPs, a celebrated master of hounds and a prominent member of the Royal Family.

Whilst we welcome donations, the main way in which you can help is by assisting us with one of our current research projects.

The nature of this particular experiment will be to determine whether the consumption of laxatives can neutralise the build-up of waste gases in the colon. As a sufferer yourself, you must know how uncomfortable and embarrassing it can be to pass wind in a public place and we feel sure that you would appreciate the value of this experiment despite the minor discomfort it might cause.

The progamme will last for a week, during which time you will consume a specially tailored diet alternating between high-fibre foods and laxatives; during this time your bodily functions will be carefully monitored and assessed.

Thank you for helping us with the research. We will call round with the diet and brief you more fully next Friday morning.

Yours sincerely

Clinical Project Manager

Duende
2, Portmeirion Street
London SW14 TL4

Telephone: 01-490 0688
or 071-490 0688

Date as postmark

Dear Sir,

I am writing to you with regard to a business proposition which I hope you will find highly attractive.

You may have read some of my books. I am the author of, among others, *Don't Go Inside!*, *Satan In Suburbia* and *Hell Lives At Number 14* and specialise in documenting true ghost stories in the British Isles. You will probably understand why I am writing to you now.

No doubt the estate agent told you the full history of your property and about the 'Fenton' stranglings and subsequent 'disturbances'. I have already interviewed the previous three owners, all of whom quickly sold up, and have obtained their permission to use their accounts of the haunting in my new book in exchange for a percentage of royalties due.

I would like to interview you at some point in the near future to discuss your own experiences and to negotiate a financial settlement for your assistance. As national serialisation and TV rights have already been sold, your co-operation in making the property accessible to journalists and other interested parties would be appreciated.

I'll telephone you one evening next week to make an appointment to visit.

Yours faithfully

Robbie Trainton

FREELANCE WRITER

NATIONAL CLEARING BANKS
DATA CENTRE

4 Cinderbridge Trade Estate, Cinderbridge Road, London SW7 TL4.
Telephone: 01-490 0688
or 071-490 0688

Date as postmark

Dear Sir/Madam

We regret to inform you that a recent computer malfunction at the Data Centre has resulted in a number of personal account records inadvertently erased.

Yours was unfortunately amongst these and, because of this error, we are having to estimate the current balance of your bank account.

Our estimate is based upon transactions carried out over the last twelve months. The last recorded balance for your account is used as the base figure for these calculations.

Your Current Account balance has been estimated at: **£ 5 . 23**

If you dispute this figure and can supply documentary evidence to this effect, please contact your bank. We will then begin action to consider your claim.

We apologise for any inconvenience.

Yours sincerely

Data Processing Manager

Sizzlers Naughty Novelties
Ltd

4th Floor, 190 Manbone Place,
London SW10 TL4

Telephone: 01-490 0688
or 071-490 0688

Dear Sir/Madam

Thank you very much for inviting us to hold a Sizzlers Naughty Novelty party at your workplace!

At a Sizzlers party, you're guaranteed a great time with your friends at work - and the opportunity to peruse and buy some of our naughty 'Adult' novelties.

Our Party Girl will show you a host of spicy treats including:

* 'Raging Bull' get-it-up cream (great for any MD who's 'a bit past it')
* 'Jumping Joy-Eggs' (brill for the bored secretary!)
* 'Good Vibrations' vibrating Y-fronts (ideal for the sales rep on those long car journeys between calls!)
* 'Mr Munchy's Edible Undies' (business lunches will *never* be the same again!)
* 'Magnifico Spanish Fly Horny Drops' (not that the blokes in despatch need any of that, eh girls!)
* 'Mr Adonis Studded Leather Shorts' (brings a touch of 'Power Dressing' to middle management of all ages and physiques!)
* Whips! (suddenly, it's fun to be the supervisor again!)
* Saucy Strip Poker Box Game (now the directors needn't be 'board' at their next meeting!)
* Condoms of all kinds! (bring production to a grinding halt!)
* Pure velvet gloves (for the bloke in the office who *really* loves himself)
* 'Fun Thongs' (great for those *dictation* sessions!)
* 'Stay firm' rubber splints (for the manager who *can't* . . .)
* The *Kama Sutra* picture book (improve *your* position in the office!)
- AND MUCH, MUCH MORE!!!!

Your Sizzlers Party Girl will be calling at your workplace on
_____ at _____ am/pm

Have fun!

Yours

Regional Sales Manager

UK BOXING FEDERATION
Founded 1874

32 Tiptree Street
London EC10 RT3.
Telephone: 01-490 0688
or 071-490 0688

TO:

Dear Sir

I am sure you will be delighted to learn that the management
of Mr Mike Tyson have asked us to contact you with regard to a
possible World Heavyweight Challenge fight, scheduled for 1991
in Atlantic City, New Jersey.

It seems that they were very impressed with your recent KO of
'Killer' Joe Morano in Mexico City last month and have been
keeping an eye on you since your outstanding points win over
Errol 'The Terminator' Higgs.

We also have it on good authority that Mr Tyson himself was
extremely annoyed at the controversial points decision when
you lost to Lars 'Mighty Thor' Jansen in Manila last year.

It is an honour that the reigning World Heavyweight Champion
believes that he has at last found a worthy contender. We have
no doubt whatsoever that you are British boxing's finest hope
to bring the title home, and we have telexed Mr Tyson's
management, on your behalf, with your acceptance.

We'll be calling on you in person in the next few days with a
representative from Mr Tyson's management to discuss terms.

Yours sincerely

Secretary

RICHTER EMPLOYMENT

A division of Robinson-Finch Employment PLC

15th Floor, St Patrick's Tower, Hillburn Street, London WC2 TT4.
Telephone: 01-490 0688 or 071-490 0688

Date as postmark

Dear Sir/Madam

RE:

The above-named person currently in your employment has applied for the following job vacancy represented by this agency:

REFUSE OPERATIVE, BARNET DEPARTMENT OF PUBLIC SANITATION

Could you please supply a reference, commenting on your employee's suitability for the above post, together with information on his/her employment history with your company and any other information you may consider relevant. All information supplied is, of course, in the strictest confidence.

Thank you for your help in this matter.

RICHTER EMPLOYMENT

A division of Robinson-Finch Employment PLC

15th Floor, St Patrick's Tower, Hillburn Street, London WC2 TT4.
Telephone: 01-490 0688 or 071-490 0688

Date as postmark

Dear Sir/Madam

RE:

The above-named person currently in your employment has applied for the following job vacancy represented by this agency:

SENIOR COACH, BRITISH LIONS RUGBY SQUAD

Could you please supply a reference, commenting on your employee's suitability for the above post, together with information on his/her employment history with your company and any other information you may consider relevant. All information supplied is, of course, in the strictest confidence.

Thank you for your help in this matter.

U.K.
AIRPORTS
CONTROL
AUTHORITY

19/41 Hinkley Street, London WC2 TL4.

Telephone: 01-490 0688 or 071-490 0688

Date as postmark

Dear Sir/Madam

From ticketing records we note you are a regular air traveller with no previous record of customs misdemeanours. As such we are pleased to issue you with this GREEN CHANNEL PASS CERTIFICATE.

These are being issued on a strictly limited basis in a six-month experiment to increase the speed at which travellers pass through customs, prior to 1992.

As a regular traveller, you will appreciate the value of being able to clear customs quickly with no inconvenient delays, and we thank you for participating in this trial study by using your pass certificate at the next available opportunity.

GREEN CHANNEL PASS CERTIFICATE

> INSERT
> PASSPORT
> PHOTOGRAPH
> HERE

Name of bearer

Insert your passport number here

To the traveller
Presentation of this certificate as you pass through the Green Channel guarantees a courteous and unhindered passage through customs.

Normal signature:

There is no limit to the number of occasions this certificate may be used within the six months of its validity.

To the Customs Officer
Please allow the bearer of this certificate to pass unchallenged through the Green Channel.

U.K.
AIRPORTS
CONTROL
AUTHORITY

Conditions of use
This certificate may only be used by the holder indicated above. It is not transferable.

Issued by the U.K. Airports Control Authority

✂

CENTRAL LIBRARY RESERVATION SERVICE

Dear

TITLE: <u>DO-IT-YOURSELF DIVORCE</u>
AUTHOR: <u>SCHWARB J & RICHARDS, M.B</u>
CAT REF: <u>ERM/209/3</u>

The above book is now ready for collection at your local library. Please collect it within the next seven days, to ensure that others wanting to read the same book are not kept waiting.

In the case of any enquiry, please ring 01-490 0688 or 071-490 0688

CENTRAL LIBRARY RESERVATION SERVICE

Dear

TITLE: <u>WHEN I'M UNFAITHFUL, I FEEL GUILTY</u>
AUTHOR: <u>LENNOX J.W., ROGERS C.B. & HAWK D.</u>
CAT REF: <u>SELF HELP, NON-FICTION</u>

The above book is now ready for collection at your local library. Please collect it within the next seven days, to ensure that others wanting to read the same book are not kept waiting.

In the case of any enquiry, please ring 01-490 0688 or 071-490 0688

CENTRAL LIBRARY RESERVATION SERVICE

Dear

TITLE: <u>THE JOYS OF POLYGAMY</u>
AUTHOR: <u>MASON, C.</u>
CAT REF: <u>NON-FICTION</u>

The above book is now ready for collection at your local library. Please collect it within the next seven days, to ensure that others wanting to read the same book are not kept waiting.

In the case of any enquiry, please ring 01-490 0688 or 071-490 0688

CENTRAL LIBRARY RESERVATION SERVICE

Dear

TITLE: <u>LIVING WITH A PIG</u>
AUTHOR: <u>CHARLOTTE, W.</u>
CAT REF: <u>SELF-HELP, NON-FICTION</u>

The above book is now ready for collection at your local library. Please collect it within the next seven days, to ensure that others wanting to read the same book are not kept waiting.

In the case of any enquiry, please ring 01-490 0688 or 071-490 0688

STARR FILMS
—— LIMITED ——
DOCUMENTARY FILMING AND POST-PRODUCTION
The Old Quarterdeck, Guevara Street, Camden, London NW1 TL4.
Telephone: 01-490 0688 or 071-490 0688

Dear

We are now in receipt of your completed consent form and are ready to begin filming *Down the Hatch*, the definitive TV documentary about the human digestive system.

As you know from our previous discussions, we aim to use time-lapse filming techniques to follow a piece of food from consumption all the way through the complex human digestive system, until it is expelled as waste.

Only very recently has it been possible for micro-cameras to probe so deeply inside the body.

The crew will be arriving next Thursday morning at about 10.00 as arranged. Please remember that you mustn't eat anything for twelve hours previously. Before we start filming, our medical advisor will administer your pain relief and once this is working, filming can commence. The doctor will be on hand to ensure that this takes place with as minimal discomfort to you as possible.

Once the food has been swallowed, the camera (with integral miniature halogen-lighting) and cable will be lowered down your throat into the alimentary canal, controlling the rate of descent by hand. Once in your stomach, the food and equipment will be moved along by natural muscular contractions into your small intestine, up into the ascending colon, along the transverse colon, down the descending colon and into the rectum.

Here, the food and camera will be expelled as waste; the camera to be recovered for future use.

Once again, thank you very much for your consent. We look forward to seeing you next week, at what, I'm sure, will be a milestone in filming and medicine.

Yours sincerely

Director

DEPARTMENT OF
ENVIRONMENTAL HEALTH

4th Floor, Oxbridge Buildings, Oxbridge Street, London WC2 TA1.
Telephone: 01-490 0688 or 071-490 0688 Ext 912

Date as postmark

Dear Sir/Madam

We are writing to all cat owners on our records to remind them that, as from the first of next month, it will become illegal to keep a cat as a pet without a licence.

You will no doubt have seen the recent press advertisements, giving details of the introduction of this licence to bring the UK in line with European Community law and to help prevent the potential spreading of rabies after 1992.

When the licence is issued, you will receive a metal collar tag with its own unique identification number, issued by our central computer. Your pet is required to wear this tag at all times.

Failure to comply with this requirement is a criminal offence. Mobile patrols will summarily check all cats; any not displaying the official tag will be impounded and may face being put down.

If you have already applied for and received a licence, please ignore this letter. If you have not, and possess (or are thinking of possessing) a cat, licences can be obtained over the counter from your local post office. Ask for form FL/542.

Thanking you for your co-operation

Administration Controller

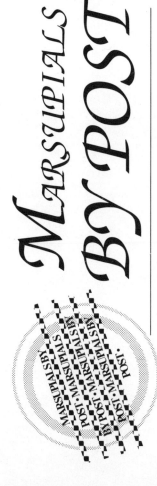

MARSUPIALS
BY POST

Unit 10, Cinderbridge Industrial Estate, Battersea, London SW11 TL4
Telephone: 01-490 0688 or 071-490 0688

Dear

From our records we notice that you have been in receipt of a Red-necked Wallaby on approval for the past six weeks. Our terms are strictly 28 days sale or return and we would therefore be grateful if you would either settle the invoice note enclosed with your marsupial, or else return it by first-class parcel post.

We regret that, until this matter has been settled, we will be unable to despatch the Koala you requested on approval from our last news sheet.

Please give this matter your most urgent attention, if you wish to continue with the pleasure and convenience of shopping for your marsupials from the comfort of your armchair, and to take full advantage of our forthcoming 'Platypus Price Pandemonium' sale.

Yours sincerely

Managing Director

BONADVENTURE TURF
ACCOUNTANTS AND
BOOKMAKERS PLC

National Offices:
18/22 Longburn Street,
London EC2 TT4.

Telephone: 01-490 0688 or
071-490 0688

Dear Sir/Madam

I am writing to confirm to you that Bonadventure PLC have decided to accept your bet, as detailed in your initial telephone call and letter of confirmation received last week.

Bonadventure PLC are currently offering odds of 19,700-1 against intelligent life being discovered on Jupiter or one of its ten satellite moons before 1 January 1992.

We confirm that we will accept your home as the stake for your bet that intelligent life WILL be discovered before that date, and your payout, should intelligent life be discovered before the aforementioned date, will be in direct proportion to the market value of your property at that date.

This bet is now fully valid in law, having been accepted by both parties, and may not be terminated at any future date between now and 1 January 1992.

With your permission, we would like to turn the details of your bet over to the company handling our public relations, so that they can announce it to the national media. Please give me a ring to confirm whether or not you would like this publicity. All bets are, of course, held in the strictest confidence unless we are otherwise instructed.

Thank you for placing your wager with Bonadventure.

With the assurance of our most prompt service at all times,

Yours sincerely

Senior Accounts Manager

F A X
BROADGATE LEGAL ADVICE CENTRE

Telephone: 01-490 0688 or 071-490 0688

Open 9.30 - 6.00 pm. Mon - Fri. 10.00 - 2.00 pm. Sat.

To:

Date:

Number of Pages:

Thank you for your recent letter detailing your employment problems. Because of the apparent seriousness of the situation, we are taking the liberty of faxing this reply in order to expedite matters.

We have studied all the allegations made about your immediate superior, and in answer to the questions raised in your letter:

1. Yes, the act you describe would be classed as sexual harassment, even though it was carried out with his feet.

2. Although we have not had sight of your contract of employment we cannot believe that your normal duties include staying behind after hours to look for missing invoices that 'may or may not have fallen down your boss's trousers', despite what you might have been told.

3. Neither can we believe that it is company policy to use the stationery store for dictation, with or without the lights on.

4. It is completely irrelevant which type of undergarments you choose to wear to your place of employment. Being told that 'stockings and suspenders are compulsory' along with 'cami-knickers', 'saucy garters', 'thigh-length boots' and 'nursing bras' is utter nonsense.

5. Disciplinary action, by law, necessitates the use of well-established procedures of verbal and written warnings. Despite what you might have been told, 'corporal punishment administered by a black leather glove' does not figure anywhere in current industrial law.

From all the information given it looks certain that you have an 'open and shut' case against your boss. Please let us know what further action you wish to take.

Yours sincerely

Legal Executive

Department of Planning and Development

National Offices: AMC Buildings,
87 Oxbridge Road,
London W1 TL4.

Telephone: 01-490 0688 or
071-490 0688 X 615

Dear Householder
RE: Forthcoming change of road name

Please note that your council has successfully applied for the registered name of your road to be duly changed.

From the first of next month, your road is to be renamed 'N'Badingi Rabombo Road' in honour of the celebrated SWAPO freedom fighter. Please advise all correspondents of this fact, as mail will cease to be delivered to addresses bearing the old road name within sixty days. Your postcode remains unaltered.

In line with policy, a full festival will accompany the name change. This will include the appearance at the unveiling ceremony of the mayor, the secretary of works and the genuine M26 tank destroyer astride which N'Badingi led the victorious masses into M'Puto in 1967. A ceremonial salute will be fired at 1 pm precisely. Other events will include community arts work-shops, face painting, alternative lesbian mime and displays of dance.

In a wider context, further changes are now in the process of being made to municipal properties. All enquiries and references to your local library must be addressed to the 'Oshogbo Free Workers Bibliotheque' and the swimming baths will, from the first of next month, be renamed the 'Fidel Castro Nuclear-Free Collective Bathing Area'. The war memorial is to be erased and will be duly rededicated to all those who selflessly gave their lives in the cause of West African liberation. Those wishing to pay their respects on future remembrance days (which will now take place on 1 May) should note that the M'paza (or 'Bird of Paradise' flower) is the correct and official token of mourning.

Yours

Executive Planning Officer

National Committee for Health and Hygiene in Schools

National Offices: 45 Wellard Road, London NW3 TL4

Telephone: 01-490 0688 or 071-490 0688 Ext 4

Date as postmark

Dear

I am writing to inform you that your son has recently been in trouble with his school authorities for performing acts of a gross personal nature while in the cubicles of his school toilets, and his case has been referred to us for further action.

While society today takes a somewhat lax view of such practices, and they may almost be regarded as just 'a natural part of growing up' in some quarters, there is still a considerable body of medical evidence which strongly suggests that such activity can be responsible for the development of schizophrenia and *Myopia extremis*, among other conditions.

With this in mind, we would strongly suggest that you take action now to curb these practices and would recommend that, at the very minimum, you take the following steps:

1. Insist on your son taking a cold shower before bed every night.
2. Check regularly under the mattress for dubious reading material.
3. Sew up the hole in his pyjama bottoms.
4. Warn him of the proven medical consequences.
5. Try to get him to sleep with his arms/hands outside the sheets.
6. Baths should be no longer than three minutes in duration - during which time the door should be left wide open.
7. The above should also apply to toilet visits.
8. All kleenex and toilet tissue should be kept under lock and key - and only dispensed under the strictest supervision.
9. Underwear inspections should be conducted on a daily basis for signs of crispness or staining.
10. Regular searches should be conducted in your son's bedroom for materials of an erotic nature.
11. If nocturnal practices persist, insist that he sleeps with a pair of oven gloves on.
12. Discourage him from indulging in any complementary practices, such as train-spotting or stamp-collecting.

Should you wish to take this matter further with a qualified member of staff, please do not hesitate to contact us on the number above.

Yours sincerely

Chief Physician (Pathological)

THE NATIONAL ASSOCIATION OF MEDIEVAL ARCHAEOLOGY

National Headquarters:
Greengage Buildings,
15/17 Greengage Road,
London W4 TL4.

Telephone: 01-490 0688
or 071-490 0688

Date as postmark

Dear Sir or Madam

I am writing to you to ask your permission to conduct a preliminary archaeological survey of limited size upon your property.

As you are no doubt aware from the deeds to your property, your present dwelling is sited some thirty-five feet above an early fourteenth-century plague burial pit which, to our knowledge, has never been excavated for purposes of historical investigation.

Many of the estimated 10,000 corpses interred beneath your property would have been buried with all their possessions, to prevent the further dissemination of the Black Death, and thus a charnel pit of this magnitude is, we feel confident, sure to lead to important new discoveries about everyday life in the fourteenth century.

If you agree to us conducting a preliminary site survey, we would propose to sink a shaft through your living-room floor into the direct centre of the pit and then retrieve a number of corpses and their possessions to check upon their relative condition. All complete or partial cadavers and/or objects would of course be removed from your home as soon as they have been properly examined, tagged and catalogued.

You will, should you agree, receive full compensation from the society for any inconvenience or structural alterations conducted, and you should be aware that there is absolutely no danger of infection, as the plague baccilli will have long since perished.

I look forward to receiving your reply to this matter at your earliest convenience.

Yours sincerely

Chief Site Officer

THE COMMITTEE FOR PSYCHIATRIC CARE IN THE COMMUNITY

National Office: AMM Buildings, St Adrian's Lane, London SW17 TT4. Telephone: 01-490 0688 or 071-490 0688

Ref: B.MC/421/B4ON

Dear

I am writing to confirm your telephone call this morning, offering to provide short term 'half-way' lodging to a patient returning to the community after a stay in a psychiatric institution.

With NHS funding for proper psychiatric care running at an all-time low, many patients in varying states of health are being ejected from health facilities with little preparation for the outside world - and that is where the work of volunteers like yourself comes in, providing homes for often severely confused people who would otherwise have nowhere to live and no-one to help them come to terms with the world.

In the first instance, we will be referring Barney McCabe to you this Wednesday at 10 am. Forgive our haste in placing this patient, but it is indicative of our current plight.

Barney is forty-one and is suffering from a number of complex psychiatric disorders, which lead him to fits of depression and torpor alternating with frenetic activity. However, none of the above disorders is deemed serious enough by the NHS to warrant confining him to an institution any longer. I am sure you will find him an exceptionally amiable house guest if you follow some simple rules.

1. Never let him see chocolate digestive biscuits. *This is most important.*

2. The same applies to any LPs by Rosemary Clooney or Helen Shapiro.

3. If he attempts to swallow any kitchen utensil, reprimand him immediately.

4. Barney has a number of irrational phobias. Try to avoid mentioning Shake 'N' Vac, Lawrence of Arabia, ears, termites, The Muppet Babies, panty hose, yellow paint, The National Theatre or Mississippi Mud Pie if he is within earshot.

cont.

5. Should Barney not respond to your commands, try addressing him as 'Your Satanic Majesty' and offering him some marmite. Failing that, *you should contact your local police station immediately.*

6. Barney enjoys painting his feet bright colours, and you should try to display positive enthusiasm for his efforts in this direction.

7. If you have a pet, do not leave them alone in the same room, as Barney can become 'over-demonstrative' in his affections if not checked.

8. Barney has been taught that it is wrong to masturbate in public, and there is no reason why you should have to tolerate this behaviour, should it resurface.

Barney will be escorted to your home by a qualified social worker who will brief you on his case in greater detail, and who will remain on call to assist you throughout Barney's stay.

As I said on the phone this morning, we are exceptionally grateful that you have volunteered to work with our organisation and I am sure that you will come to derive a great deal of personal satisfaction from helping patients re-integrate with society.

Don't hesitate to contact me if I can be of any further assistance.

Kind regards

Chief Regional Placement Officer

THE BOSCOMBE HOME FOR ABANDONED DOGS

Caring for Strays since 1955

Cinderbridge Estate, off Cinderbridge Road, London EC14 TL4. Telephone:01-490 0688 or 071-490 0688

Date as postmark

Dear Animal Lover

Thank you for responding to our recent 'Adopt-A-Dog' appeal.

It is now only two weeks before the Boscombe Home has to close and we were becoming worried that some of the larger dogs in our care would not find new homes and have to be put down. This was, sadly, especially true in the case of 'Genghis'.

Although loveable, his size and unpredictable temperament have made him unsuitable as a pet for many of the people who have taken dogs from us. This, coupled with the recent bad publicity surrounding un-neutered male rottweilers, meant that we had virtually given up hope of someone wanting to adopt him.

Imagine our delight, then, when your letter arrived offering to re-house 'Genghis' for us. Everything in your letter - your half-acre garden surrounded by an eight-foot chain link fence, your experience handling big cats at Sark Zoo and the fact that there are no small children in the vicinity - proves that you'll be the perfect new owner.

'Genghis' and his handlers will arrive next Sunday morning at 10.00 am as requested in your letter. They'll hand him over and give you full details of his raw meat diet and the course of enemas that has to be continued for another two weeks until his tape worm is cured.

Thanking you once again for your kind offer. I know 'Genghis' will take to you in exactly the same way as he's taken to his five handlers here at the home in the past six months.

Yours sincerely

Owner, The Boscombe Home For Abandoned Dogs